CONCILIUM

Religion in the Seventies

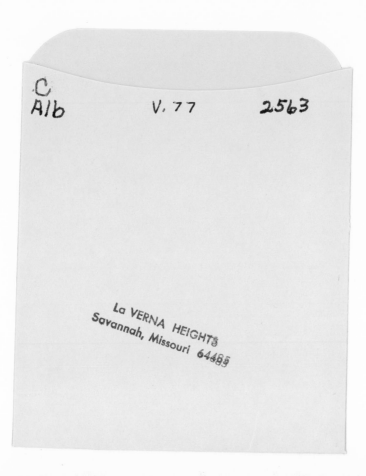

CONCILIUM
Religion in the Seventies

Volume 77: Church History

ELECTION AND CONSENSUS
IN THE CHURCH

Edited by

Giuseppe Alberigo
and Anton Weiler

Herder and Herder

1972
HERDER AND HERDER NEW YORK
1221 Avenue of the Americas,
New York 10020

Cum approbatione Ecclesiastica

Library of Congress Catalog Card Number: 72–3942
Copyright © 1972 by Herder and Herder, Inc. and Stichting Concilium.
All rights reserved. Nothing contained in this publication shall be reproduced
and/or made public by means of print, photographic print, microfilm, or in
any other manner without the previous consent of the Stichting Concilium
and the publishers.

Printed in the United States

CONTENTS

PART I
ARTICLES

Rudolf Schnackenburg

Community Co-operation in the New Testament

HOW can lay people (the majority of the people of God) share, in full co-responsibility, in the decisions of the Church? This is one of the most urgent questions confronting Christians today; any attempt to answer it in the light of the New Testament must be based on examination of the special relationships prevailing when the Church was founded.

The risen Lord had given full power to the apostles to proclaim the Gospel, and they were the first to call the Christian communities into being. Their own call gave them a very special position in the early communities, although, being active in missionary work, they did not live permanently in those local communities, and so did not act as leaders in the way that others were able to do later in the history of the Church. The early communities had to evolve their own way of life and to create their own structures for this purpose. The communities were differently structured and organized. There was relatively little contact between them, and so considerable pluriformity. In some, those with charismatic gifts provided the necessary services. In others, those who would "labour" among their brothers (see 1 Thess. 5. 12) had to be found to devote their time and strength to local problems. Because each community was so distinctive, it is difficult to find a common denominator for the life and attitude of them all.

Our knowledge is very incomplete. Paul's letters offer only an imperfect insight into his relationship with the communities he established, and our main source of information concerning the community at Jerusalem is open to suspicion because—imperceptibly—the author of the Acts of the Apostles included in his account the relationships prevailing in his own times.[1] All the other written material is early post-apostolic and therefore cannot give us satisfactory answers. But we can venture a few comments which may help us to draw some cautious conclusions with a bearing on the present problem. Although we should really begin with the letters of Paul, which are earlier in date and more reliable, I have decided to consider first the evidence in Acts, because of the importance of the "primitive" community of Jerusalem for the present question.

I. The Primitive Community of Jerusalem

Before Pentecost, Matthias was elected as one of the twelve to replace Judas at a meeting of the community. He was not freely chosen by the members of the community, but, by "casting lots", was elected by the Lord (Acts 1. 15–26). Several aspects of this account, which was shaped by the author (Peter's address), but not freely devised by him (the two candidates named), are, however, worth noting. Peter assembles not only the other members of the circle of twelve,[2] but also all the "brethren ... about a hundred and twenty",[3] so that all the believers, including women

[1] Comparatively little attention has been given to questions of authorhip and editing, despite a great deal of research into the literary character of Acts. Some critical comments will be found in E. Haenchen, *Die Apostelgeschichte* (H. A. W. Meyers Kommentarwerk, 12th impression) (Göttingen, 1959), and H. Conzelmann, *Die Apostelgeschichte (Handbuch zum Neuen Testament, 7)* (Tübingen, 1963); A. Lemaire is moderately critical and very helpful in *Les ministères aux origines de l'église* (Paris, 1971), pp. 45–71; see also R. Schnackenburg, "Lukas als Zeuge verschiedener Gemeindestrukturen", in *Bibel und Leben*, 12 (1971), pp. 232–47.

[2] The notion that the circle of twelve was constituted before the Easter event has undergone a good deal of criticism; nevertheless, I support it; see B. Rigaux, "Die 'Zwölf' in Geschichte und Kerygma", in H. Ristow and K. Matthiae (Eds.), *Der historische Jesus und der kerygmatische Christus* (Berlin, 1960), pp. 468–86; J. Giblet, "Les Douze. Histoire et théologie", *Aux origines de l'Église* (Recherches Bibliques VII) (Bruges, 1965), pp. 51–64; A. Vögtle, *Lexikon für Theologie und Kirche*, 2X (Freiburg im Breisgau, 1965), col. 1443 ff.; J. Roloff, *Apostolat—Verkündigung—Kirche* (Gütersloh, 1965), pp. 138–68.

[3] According to the Mishnah Sanhedrin I 6 e, a hundred and twenty Jews were required to form a synedrion in a town, see S. Krauss, *San-*

(see 1. 14), take part. They are told why the election is held, nominate two candidates (or at least consent to the nomination[4]) and acknowledge the result as the Lord's decision. The whole unique process can hardly have been invented by the author. Memory of Jesus' having chosen from his disciples "twelve, whom he named apostles" (Luke 6. 13) undoubtedly played a part here, but choice by casting lots, which was a common Jewish practice in the temple cult,[5] points, together with the names, to a Jewish-Christian tradition.

The sharing of the whole community in the appointment of the seven in Act 6. 1–6 is even more clearly revealed. The "seven" were certainly not simply chosen to look after the poor, but, like the "apostles", had the task of proclaiming the word as independent leaders of the Jewish-Hellenistic group in the community of Jerusalem.[6] The author seems to place these seven men under the authority of the apostles (6. 6), but in his report attempts to reconcile any possible tensions. He also states explicitly that the "twelve" summoned an assembly of all the brothers (6. 2) and proposed that the seven should be nominated (6. 3). The whole community consented to the appointment and chose the seven, who were then named (6. 5). This is a clear case of co-operation by consensus and choice.

The "Council of Jerusalem" (Acts 15) followed a somewhat different course. The delegates from the predominantly gentile community at Antioch, Paul and Barnabas (15. 3), were welcomed by the community and "the apostles and elders" in Jeru-

---

hedrin—Makkot (Giessen, 1933), pp. 91 ff.; the number given in Acts cannot, however, be explained by this: see H. Conzelmann, *ad loc.* Luke might have been thinking of ten times the number "twelve"; this can be compared with the opinion of Rabbi Nechemja in Sanhedrin I 6 e. For the historicity and theological themes in Acts 1. 15–26, see K. Rengstorf, "Die Zuwahl des Matthias", in *Studia Theologica*, 15 (1961), pp. 35–67.

[4] ἔστησαν (Acts 1. 23) refers to Peter's address to all the brothers assembled (1. 15). A second version in the singular (D gig. Aug.) confines the nomination of the candidates to Peter.

[5] See P. Billerbeck, *Kommentar zum Neuen Testament aus Talmud und Midrasch*, II (Munich, 1924), pp. 596 ff.

[6] K. H. Rengstorf, *Theologisches Wörterbuch zum Neuen Testament*, II (Stuttgart, 1935), p. 630; P. Gaechter, *Die Sieben. Petrus und seine Zeit* (Innsbruck, 1958), pp. 105–54; J. H. Bihler, *Die Stephanusgeschichte* (Munich, 1963), pp. 192–216; E. Haenchen, *op. cit.*, pp. 218–22; A. Lemaire, *op. cit.*, p. 57.

salem (15. 4), but some converts from Judaism demanded that the gentile Christians should be circumcised (15. 5). This was, of course, a question of the utmost importance for the future of the mission. The council was composed of "apostles and elders" (15. 6, 22, 23). Is the author simply recording his own views here, or are we to give credence to what he says, especially from the historical point of view?

It is not clear what part the "apostles" played in the community of Jerusalem: only Peter and James spoke at the council. The "elders" or "presbyters", however, are especially interesting. Although Luke says that such presbyters were appointed in Paul's communities (14. 23), this statement cannot be historically correct, at least as a title for the office these men occupied, because Paul does not tell us about "presbyters"; it is therefore possible that the author of *Acts* used a word current in his own period and environment for an office in the community of Jerusalem.

There are, however, serious counter-arguments. The office of "elder" was a very old Jewish institution. The elders were representatives of the "community of the Lord", which had, the Jews believed, to regulate its own affairs.[7] It is possible, then, that the "Hebrews" in the community of Jerusalem also chose representatives on the model of the "Hellenists".[8] Certainly these "elders" do not feature very prominently in *Acts*. Although they are only mentioned once later with James (21. 18), they have the important task of persuading Paul to dissipate the growing mistrust of his teaching by accepting the four Nazarites (21. 20–26). It appears that the "elders" supported James here, acting as an authoritative consultative body with the power of taking joint decisions. It is possible, therefore, that the author mentioned the "apostles" summarily in Acts 15, but that the circle of the twelve was already in the course of breaking up, while a new structure

[7] For the history of this institution, see G. Bornkamm, *Theologisches Wörterbuch zum Neuen Testament*, VI (Stuttgart, 1959), pp. 655–62; A. Lemaire, *op. cit.*, pp. 21–7; for the historicity of the "elders" in the community of Jerusalem, see H. Freiherr von Campenhausen, *Kirchliches Amt und geistliche Vollmacht in den ersten drei Jahrhunderten* (Tübingen, ²1963), pp. 83 ff.

[8] P. Gaechter, *op. cit.*, pp. 133 ff., is of this opinion—at least he certainly thinks that the "twelve" appointed these men: "In keeping with the election of the seven Hellenists, the twelve in all probability *also set up a college of seven men for the Hebrews*."

with James as leader and the elders as representatives of the community was already being formed in Jerusalem.

The decision not to insist on the circumcision of the gentile converts was taken by the whole assembly after James's important vote. The author says: "It seemed good to the apostles and elders, with the whole church, to choose men from among them and send them to Antioch..." (15. 22), but the decree reads simply: "The brethren, both the apostles and the elders, to the brethren ...in Antioch...greeting."[9] The second statement is more exact, because the elders were the representatives of the whole community. In any case, there can be no doubt that the whole community gave its consent, even if we refer to the passage in Gal. 2, where Paul speaks of those "who were of repute" (οἱ δοκοῦντες) or of the "pillars", James, Cephas and John, who had given their consent to the decision not to impose circumcision on the gentile converts (2.6; see also 2. 9). In the course of his argument, however, Paul stresses how important it is for his apostolate to be independent of that of the earlier apostles (πρὸ ἐμοῦ ἀποστόλους, 1. 17; see also 1. 19). The community could be included in αὐτοῖς (2. 2a) because Paul laid down his gospel before "those who were of repute" κατ᾽ ἰδίαν (2. 2b).[10] Although the Pauline text is in many ways not clear, we cannot conclude that the community of Jerusalem was not asked to give its consent. In the Acts of the Apostles, this consensus was confirmed by sending Judas (Barsabbas) and Silas, "leading men among the brethren", to Antioch (15. 22).

The incomplete description of the emergence and early life of the community at Antioch in Acts 11. 19–26 and 13. 1–3 shows us that the members did more than merely hear the word of God. The second passage makes it clear that "prophets and

[9] According to one version, καὶ οἱ ἀδελφοί (see the International Greek New Testament), there were three groups—the apostles, the elders and the brothers. This version is, however, weaker than the well-testified Egyptian text. What is more, all the members of the community, including the apostles and the elders, were regarded as "brothers" (see 1. 15 ff.; 15. 7, 13, etc.).

[10] H. Schlier, *Der Brief an die Galater* (H. A. W. Meyers Kommentarwerk, 12th impression) (Göttingen, 1962), pp. 66 ff. Schlier believes that the decision was made, not by the whole church, but only by the δοκοῦντες; on p. 115, however, he admits that the community gave its consent. See also E. Haenchen, *op. cit.*, p. 406.

teachers" led the community, and that the author had at his disposal a list of five names, beginning with Barnabas and ending with Saul (Paul). These five men gave the impetus to further missionary activity, probably by their prophetic voices, but when the author says that Barnabas and Paul were sent out, we have certainly to think of the whole community as present. Luke no doubt assumed this, although the wording of 13. 3 makes it apparent that it was those charismatic men who, after fasting, praying and laying on hands, sent the missionaries out. On their return, those sent out gave a report to the whole community about what they had done (14. 27). The fact that the decision made at Jerusalem was conveyed to the community of Antioch to some extent confirms one's suspicion that the mission was supported by the whole community. In Paul's account, the part played by the community is obscured by the apostle's own personal intentions, but it does emerge to some extent in the agreement made between the three "pillars" of the community of Jerusalem on the one hand, and Paul and Barnabas as representatives of the Antiochian community on the other (Gal. 2. 9).[11]

II. THE PAULINE COMMUNITIES

Despite his strong missionary sense and personal commitment, as the "apostle of Jesus Christ", Paul in no way assumed a position of leadership over the communities he had established that excluded all right to participate in decisions. He saw his office as a "ministry of reconciliation", believing that he was only an "ambassador for Christ", and that God made an appeal through him to the community (2 Cor. 5. 18–21). In Paul's view, those who proclaim the Gospel are servants through whom the Corinthians, for example, came to believe (1 Cor. 3. 5), and their only task is to build up the community as "God's temple" (1 Cor. 3. 10–17). Paul uses the image of the birth of a child to describe how he is "in labour" and how Christ is "formed" in the community (Gal. 4. 19). Elsewhere, he "admonishes" the Corinthians like a father (1 Cor. 4. 14 f.). Without relinquishing his full power (2 Cor. 10. 8; 13. 10), he aims above all to lead the com-

[11] E. Haenchen, op. cit., pp. 407 ff., stresses this viewpoint.

munity to maturity (1 Cor. 3. 1–3; 14. 20; Phil. 3. 15), so that
the members can manage their own affairs and make responsible
decisions.

The importance that Paul attached to self-determination or,
at least, to shared responsibility in the community is clearly revealed in cases of conflict. He himself judged the case of the in-
cestuous man (1 Cor. 5), deciding that such an offender could
not be tolerated in the community (5. 3, 13). The disciplinary
action, however, has to be carried out in such a way that the
Corinthians should assemble with the spirit of the absent Paul
present among them and, "with the power of the Lord Jesus",
deliver this man to Satan for the destruction of the flesh" (5. 4).
The syntax of the passage is not clear,[12] but it is obvious that Paul
does not want to act in isolation from the rest of the community,
but wants the consent of the other members. Indeed, he wants
them to come to this decision themselves and to carry out the
action. This is only one example of Paul's attempt to obtain a
real consensus between himself and the community, a consensus
with the "power of the Lord Jesus" behind it.

Another example in 1 Cor. is Paul's suggestion that the community should choose a fellow member to act as judge between
brothers, so that scandalous lawsuits might be avoided (1 Cor.
6. 5). He does not name a man himself, but leaves it to the community to accept his suggestion and to choose someone. He
would be happier if the appointment were not necessary, and
the brothers were prepared to forgo their right (6. 7 ff.). Paul
expresses his opinion quite openly and clearly in all questions
concerning life in the community about which he is consulted,
but lays down no strict directions. When asked, for instance,
whether women should not wear a veil in public worship (1 Cor.
11. 2–16), he concludes a lengthy argument by saying "judge for
yourselves" (11. 13) and by pointing to the practice in the
"churches of God" (11. 16). We may therefore presume to say
that he leaves the final decision to the community. Although he

[12] H. Conzelmann, *Der erste Brief an die Korinther* (Göttingen, 1969),
p. 117, has explored the various possibilities of the construction, but his
statement that "the community forms the forum, but does not co-operate"
hardly seems to be in accordance with the apostle's intention. J. Weiss' interpretation, in *Der erste Korintherbrief* (Göttingen, 1910; 1970), pp. 127 ff.,
is more subtle.

gives "directions" (διατάσσεσθαι) several times (1 Cor. 7. 13; 11. 34; 16. 1), this does not mean that all participation on the part of the community is excluded. The well-known commandment that "women should keep silence in the churches" (1 Cor. 14. 33b–36), which is contradictory to 1 Cor. 11. 5, is probably an interpolation.[13]

We have no precise knowledge about the way in which the communities co-operated in the appointment of those holding office. It is possible that those who "laboured" among their brothers and were "over" them in the community of Thessalonica were appointed by Paul in consultation with the brothers. Paul's exhortation to acknowledge, love and esteem them "because of their work" (1 Thess. 5. 12 ff.) leaves many possible interpretations open. The many charisms present in the community of Corinth made it possible for no special office-holders to be elected. We may presume that the "bishops and deacons" at Philippi (Phil. 1. 1) were chosen by the community and that the choice may have been confirmed by Paul. This is because, in addition to Epaphrodius, Paul's "fellow worker" (2. 25–29), and perhaps other voluntary helpers (τοὺς τοιούτους, 2. 29), they give the impression of having been appointed by the community to carry out certain regular functions. But it is not possible to say precisely how they were installed.[14]

III. The Communities in the Gospel of Matthew

Any inferences that can be drawn from the gospel of Matthew concerning the Christian communities (perhaps in Syria) are of particular interest to us here. Quite apart from the promise of full power made to Peter (16. 18 ff.), a view of the community is expressed in Jesus' discourse to the disciples (Matt. 18)—basically a pastoral instruction or community "rule"[15]—which makes this

[13] This view is supported with good arguments by H. Conzelmann, *Der erste Brief an die Korinther*, pp. 289 ff.; K. Thraede, *Reallexikon für Antike und Christentum*, 8 (Stuttgart, 1970), p. 232, is of the same opinion.
[14] H. Freiherr von Campenhausen, *op. cit.*, pp. 73 ff.; J. Gnilka, *Der Philipperbrief* (Freiburg im Breisgau, 1968), pp. 35–9.
[15] W. Trilling, *Das wahre Israel. Studien zur Theologie des Matthäus—Evangeliums* (Munich, 1964), pp. 106–123; W. Pesch, "Die sogenannte Gemeindeordnung Mt 18", in *Biblische Zeitschrift*, 7 (1963), pp. 220–35; P. Bonnard, "Composition et signification historique de Matthieu XVIII",

chapter important in our context. There is, for example, in 18. 15–17, a rule on the Jewish (perhaps Qumran) model for the case of a brother who is at fault. This rule is in three stages: correction at first in private, then with two or three brothers present as witnesses, and finally before the whole community. If the sinner still refuses to obey, he must be regarded as "a gentile and a tax collector" and be avoided by his brothers. A disciplinary measure of this kind taken by the whole community (see 1 QS 6. 1) means that the community could, by common consent, come to an important decision about a fellow member. Considered in this context, the statement about binding and loosing (18. 18)—whatever it meant originally and however it came to be applied later—has to be related to the community here.[16]

Other examples in Matthew point to the fact that the community was regarded predominantly as a community of brothers (see, for example, 23. 8). Scripture scholars (13. 52) teachers and catechists (23. 10) belonged to it and may have been its leaders, although the structures are not clear, and we can only presume that all the members shared in all communal affairs in a community dominated by the idea of brotherhood.

IV. Later Developments

This idea of a community of brothers subject to the same Lord and to mutual service of each other predominated in the primitive Church. This meant that the leaders, either the apostles or else men chosen by the community because of their charismatic gifts, were so fully incorporated into the community that the community seemed to be active as a whole. It is certain that important decisions were never taken without the consent of the community. The same idea of brotherhood can be found in later texts (1 Pet. 2. 17; 5. 9; James 1. 9 ff.; 2. 1, 5, 15 ff.; 3. 1 ff.; 4. 11; 5. 9, 19 ff.; Heb. 2. 11 ff.; 3. 1, 12; 13. 22; Apoc. 1. 9; 6. 11; 19.

De Jésu aux Evangiles (Gembloux and Paris, 1967), pp. 130–40; B. Rigaux, *Témoignage de l'évangile de Matthieu* (Bruges and Paris, 1967), pp. 119–23.

[16] For the historical relationship between Matt. 18. 18 and 16. 19, see W. Trilling, *op. cit.*, pp. 156–8; G. Bornkamm, "Die Bindeund Lösegewalt in der Kirche des Matthäus", *Die Zeit Jesu*. Festschrift für H. Schlier (Freiburg im Breisgau, 1970), pp. 93-107, especially pp. 101 ff.

10; 22. 9), and it is obvious from the emphasis on brotherly love in 1 John that the same idea prevailed in the Johannine community. There is, however, also a certain emphasis on the need to follow the example and the directives of the "leaders" of the community (Heb. 13. 7, 17, 24; 1 Pet. 5. 1–5).

It is clear from Luke's writings (especially Acts 14. 23), 1 Pet. 5. 1 ff.; James 5. 14, and above all the pastoral letters, that the idea of the "presbyter" was beginning to emerge in many Christian communities, especially after about A.D. 80. These presbyters were not, as we assumed the elders in the community of Jerusalem were (see I above), mere representatives of the community. They formed an authoritative body or college of leaders,[17] who were, according to 1 Tim. 4. 14, "ordained" by the laying on of hands. The candidates had to show that they possessed certain qualities and were carefully examined (see 1 Tim. 5. 22). Those presbyters who "ruled well" were "considered worthy of double honour, especially those who labour in preaching and teaching" (5. 17). Unfortunately, we cannot tell whether the community played an active part in the selection of candidates.

As the whole emphasis in the pastoral letters is on the standing and the authority of those holding office in the community, it is hardly surprising that information about the co-operation of the community by consensus and choice is lacking. This absence of information, however, does not justify the assumption that such co-operation was excluded. In the Didache, we read: "Elect (χειροτονήσατε) episkopoi and diakonoi who are worthy of the Lord" (15. 1), which is clear evidence that the choice of office-bearers was made by the community. The prominent position of those holding office at the end of the first century may have developed, among other reasons, because of the need to refute false teaching. According to 1 John, all members of the community were exhorted to "test the spirits" (4. 1), so that false teachers would seem to have been excluded from the community by the members (2. 18–27).

[17] For the significance of the colleges of presbyters, see H. Freiherr von Campenhausen, op. cit., pp. 89–90; W. Michaelis, Das Ältestamen der christlichen Gemeinde im Licht der heiligen Schrift (Berne, 1953); G. Bornkamm, Theologisches Wörterbuch zum Neuen Testament, VI, pp. 662–8; A. Lemaire, op. cit., p. 184 (summary).

In the struggle against false teaching, however, those who held office and were committed to the sound teaching of the apostolic tradition were bound to gain in significance. This led to a development in which, from the second century onwards, the communities tended more and more to become separated into "shepherds and flocks", with an increasing stress on the "monarchical" episcopate. None the less, the co-operation and co-responsibility of the whole community, so prominent in New Testament times, were indispensable elements in the life of the Church, which must be taken even more seriously into account today. The fundamental idea of "brotherhood" has to be seen as a constant call to renewal in the Church.

Translated by David Smith

Bruno Kleinheyer

Consensus in the Liturgy

SINCE liturgical celebrations are actions of the community as a whole, involving both hierarchy and laity, the liturgy is a *locus theologicus* which always has and will reveal consensus—and dissent. Within the limits of this article I can only touch on some aspects of this immense subject, and I have been asked to try to indicate some parallels between developments in the early history of the Church and in the present. I shall not discuss preaching, even though it is an essential part of liturgy; the free homily is an essential element of the liturgical celebration,[1] and this is the area in which agreement and disagreement can most easily be expressed. Here I can only discuss the word in the form of prayer, and the liturgical sign in the widest sense. My starting-point will be some experiences of the present and the recent past, and I shall try to make connections between them and the earliest period of the Church. I shall end these "remarks" with some discussion of the area of liturgy in which there has naturally been the greatest effort to achieve consensus, the liturgy of ordination, and this will also connect this article with others in this issue.

I. LITURGICAL REFORM IN THE PRESENT

1. *Consensus and Dissent at the Beginnings of Liturgical Reform*

Since more and more people are coming to regard the reform of the liturgy as dating from the publication of the *Constitution*

---

[1] *Ordo Missae*, 14; *Institutio Generalis Missalis Romani*, 42.

on the Liturgy, it is useful to mention some of the controversies
which took place at the beginnings of the liturgical movement in
French- and German-speaking countries.[2] In the years after World
War I, neither Lambert Beauduin nor Romano Guardini would
have dared to imagine that in their lifetime a pope could describe
"zeal for the renewal of the liturgy as a sign of the workings of
divine providence and a visitation by the Holy Spirit of his
Church" (Pius XII, 22 September 1956), or that a council could
make such words its own (*Constitution on the Liturgy*, 43). On
the other hand, it is equally true that such an avowed opponent
of liturgical reform as the then bishop of Freiburg, Konrad
Gröber, would also never have envisaged a pope taking such a
position. Opposition and support were clearly revealed by a
movement which began at the grass-roots—if we must have these
categories—and was taken up by priests and laymen, regarded
with suspicion and sometimes strongly opposed by others, rejected by individual bishops and vigorously promoted by others.[3]
The recognition of the movement by a pope and a council is a
victory and the beginning of a new stage of development.

Of course, this outline of the progress of the liturgical reform
in the first half of this century must be seen in a wider context;
this makes the problem of consensus and dissent even more complex. The renewal of the liturgy did not begin after the end of
World War I, although that period was particularly fruitful—in
the same way that the difficulties of the Churches in Germany
after 1933 brought about a return to the sources. The biblical
movement, the new concentration on pastoral work among young
people and the growing ecumenical movement were connected
with the moves to renew the liturgy. All these are separate
elements in a movement for renewal within the Church whose
roots go far back into the nineteenth century; Pius X's decree on
frequent communion should rank with them.

[2] See F. Kolbe, *Die Liturgische Bewegung* (Aschaffenburg, 1964).
[3] See Th. Maas-Eward, *Liturgie und Pfarrei. Einfluss der liturgischen
Erneuerung auf Leben und Verstandnis der Pfarrei im deutschen Sprach-
gebiet* (Paderborn, 1969), esp. pp. 213-49.

2. *Consensus and Dissent in the Reception of the Post-Conciliar Liturgical Reform*

We are still in the early stages of reception of the liturgical reform inaugurated by the Council. But what do we mean by "inaugurated by the Council"? Only a comparison which is not at present possible between the attitudes of the Council members at the time of its summoning, and at the time of the final vote on the constitution on the liturgy, will show how much development from opposition to acceptance took place in the Council itself. A clear indication that the overwhelming consensus in the Council concealed a measure of dissent is given by a comparison of the first version of the *Institutio Generalis Missalis Romani* with the version published a year later with the missal itself.[4] In this context we may also recall the opposition of the societies dedicated to restoration which now came into the open as minorities.[5]

It is indisputable that the conciliar reform has found widespread support, and the liturgical books which have since appeared have been accepted. At the same time the historian will have to face the implications for the subject of consensus and dissent of the fact that within a relatively short time more than twenty-five thousand copies of an unauthorized liturgical book have been sold in German-speaking countries.[6] Of course sales figures alone do not allow conclusions about liturgical practice. We may wonder how many of these books were in use for how long, or how many were not used at all, but went straight into a bookcase. Dissent? Yes, but its extent is hard to measure—though, equally, it is only possible to give an approximate estimate of the support for post-conciliar reform. A different sort of question also comes in here: to what extent have liturgical communities in the past been, and are they now, able to express their views on liturgical texts from one source or another? The *Insti-*

[4] See E. J. Lengeling, "Die neue Ordnung der Eucharistifeier", *Lebendiger Gottesdienst* 17/18 (Münster, 1970), pp. 53 ff.

[5] See F. Henrich (ed.), *Liturgiereform im Streit der Meinung, Studien und Berichte der katholischen Akademie in Bayern* (Würzburg, 1968), esp. the essays by H. B. Meyer, E. M. de Saventhem and H. Rennings.

[6] A. Schilling, *Fürbitten und Kanongebete der holländischen Kirche* (Essen, 1968).

tutio Generalis of the reformed missal says: "The breaking of the bread has not only a practical significance, but is a sign that we all eat in the communion of the one bread of life, which is Christ, and thereby become his body (1 Cor. 10. 17)."[7] This is a clear recommendation to abandon the practice of distributing the eucharistic bread in preformed particles. If the author's experience is typical, this recommendation has received little response. It will be interesting to see how things develop. Will a consensus form here? Whatever happens, the text quoted seems to imply that this is more than a practical question, an intensification of preaching by sign: taking part in the meal means being part of the community.

3. A Lesson in Consensus: Communion in the Hand

No one will want to maintain that the Council's decision to reform the rite of the Mass included this development as a matter of course, just as it is also impossible to assert that the intention was to exclude the practice permanently. We cannot be totally precise about when and where dissent from the previously general practice first appeared, except to say in the few years after 1964 in Dutch communities. It is significant (to insert a methodological remark) that even after only five years it is difficult to be precise about the time and place where a new practice began. (That this is not a "new" practice, but a return to a long-established custom, is irrelevant to our immediate concerns.) What is remarkable is the speed with which the new form of distributing communion took hold—and the reaction of the Church leadership. The world episcopate was consulted, and although a majority were against the practice it was allowed at the request of individual bishops' conferences.[8] For many communities and for many individuals within communities this was the first stimulus to reconsider the existing practice and examine their own practice. The present picture is marked by variety. A consensus exists, to the extent that it is not the minister's business to regulate the practice of the communicant (and how much silent

[7] *Institutio Generalis,* 56c; on this see Lengeling, *loc. cit.,* p. 242.
[8] See *Notitiae* 48 (1969), pp. 347–53.

dissent exists among some ministers?), and dissent at the same time among individual communicants.

Is this also "only" a question of practice, and as such of no special importance to our inquiry? Such a classification of the question is open to objection. Must not the question, like that of the frequency of the reception of the Eucharist (Pius X's decree on communion was a delayed effect of the struggle over Jansenist rigorism), be seen in a wider context, in the context of the general reform of liturgical celebration and the revaluation of the theological aspect of the community's coming together for the liturgy (cf. *Constitution on the Liturgy*, 7)? Must we not say that in the return to the old way of distribution a new relationship between hierarchy and community is seeking expression, that it makes the character of ministry as service a little clearer? This does leave open the question of how far the choice of a new practice is a conscious one in individual cases.

II. A Look at the Past

Only someone quite unfamiliar with historical research would believe that the question of consensus and dissent in liturgical celebration, and in relation to the beliefs expressed therein, is less complex in regard to earlier periods. My example of the development of the method of distributing the Eucharist is a warning to be careful. Answers to my original question are apt to turn into a new set of questions.

We know that the community has always said its "Amen" to the priestly prayers. It gave its assent to the meaning of the celebration; it was indeed right and fitting to thank God for his saving actions in Jesus Christ. But are the acclamations prescribed in the rubrics really the only indicators of consensus and dissent? How far do the liturgical texts reflect what the community actually believes?

In Justin's time the celebrant of the liturgy made up the entire eucharistic prayer from his own resources.[9] We may assume that individual celebrants did not follow their own inclinations, but

[9] Justin Martyr, *Apologia*, 1.67: "The president in like manner offers up prayers and thanksgivings with all his might; and the people assent with *Amen*."

prayed so that the community could recognize its faith in the prayer said on behalf of all. We can demonstrate it, at least to some extent. At least in the central eucharistic prayer, which is also the main area under investigation, there is definite evidence of the celebrant's attachment to the faith of the community, to the traditional faith determined by the Scriptures. In all the different texts of the institution narrative which existed in the different liturgical areas of East and West in the various periods of the early Church—and there were far more than are or ever will be known to scholars—the common elements far outweigh the divergences.[10] In this core of the liturgy the striving for agreement with one's particular tradition and with the faith of this particular generation, and thus—explicitly or implicitly—with other churches near and far, is quite clear.

This is a first step to the formation of a canon. A stage on this path—which should not be rejected in advance as false—is the provision of a model eucharistic prayer, such as that Hippolytus gives in his *Traditio Apostolica*. He insists: "It is quite unnecessary for the bishop to use the exact words given above, as if he had to learn them by heart in order to make his thanksgiving to God. It is better for everyone to pray as best he can. . . . The only essential is that his prayer should be correct and orthodox."[11] Hippolytus only requires that the community should be able to agree—and here he speaks for all. The right to make up one's own liturgical prayers is limited by the connection with the faith of the Church. The *lex credendi* is the *lex orandi*.

It was not inevitable, but the various stages of the development make it historically intelligible, that the Hippolytan model should have become the canonized post-Tridentine Missal. The fact that the right to make up prayers remained for a long time reserved to bishops, in theory at least until the post-Tridentine reform, only seems odd if we forget that it is the bishop (within his presbyterium) and not the individual presbyter who is the real

---

[10] See F. Hamm, *Die liturgischen Einsetzungsberichte im Sinne vergleichender Liturgieforschung untersucht* (Münster, 1928).

[11] Hippolytus, *Traditio Apostolica*, 9 (Botte, 28): "*Nullo modo necessarium est, ut proferat eadem verba quae praediximus . . . sed secundum suam potestatem unusquisque oret. . . . Tantum oret quod sanum est in orthodoxia.*"

celebrant. Not that we should leave out of account the fact that this position was modified as the presbyterium gradually took over more and more of the bishop's duties as president of the liturgical celebration. The knowledge about the use of this right provided by studies of the oldest remaining volume of Roman liturgical texts, the *"Sacramentarium Veronese"*,[12] is relevant here. The desire to reformulate liturgical prayers is far from being the dominant characteristic of this first period of liturgical history about which we have any information. At least as strong is the need to rely on older texts, although no obligation to do so existed. To postulate inadequacy before the task as the only reason hardly seems to do justice to the phenomenon. Is not the desire that the prayer should be "correct and orthodox", the desire for agreement with the faith handed down to and living in the community, an element which cannot be left out of the interpretation?

N. Brox has once more revealed a striking example of dissent in liturgical practice in the early Church in his recent *Concilium* article about the first stage of the dispute about Easter between the churches of Asia Minor, for whom Polycarp emerged as spokesman, and the Roman Church under Anicetus, which must certainly have been speaking for many Western communities.[13] But however stubborn the disagreement—it flared up again after little more than a generation—the consensus was more important than the disagreement on detail.

Not every conflict had such an eirenic course, as anyone familiar with church history knows. We can pass over the deep effect on liturgical prayer, both direct and long after, of the Christological disputes which broke out violently in the third century.[14] There has for a long time been an insufficient realization that

---

[12] See A. Stuiber, *Libelli sacramentorum Romani. Untersuchungen zur Entstehung des sogenannten Sacramentarium Leonianum* (Bonn, 1950).

[13] N. Brox, "The Conflict between Anicetus and Polycarp": *Concilium*, Jan. 1972 (American edn., vol. 71). Without going into details, it seems to me that what was at issue in the question of the date was less the substance of the Easter feast—contrary to what Brox thinks—than a different evaluation of the Old Testament passover for the community of Jesus Christ.

[14] See J. A. Jungmann, "Die Abwehr des germanischen Arianismus und der Umbruch der religiösen Kultur in frühen Mittelalter", *Liturgisches Erbe und pastorale Gegenwart* (Innsbruck, 1960), pp. 3–86.

the causal connection with regard to "consensus and dissent" is not just a matter of theological discussion redirecting liturgical prayer, but the reverse; changes in devotional attitudes and consequent changes in the form and expression of liturgical celebrations give rise to new theological positions. I must refrain from going into specific questions here. The references to the connections between the disputes in eucharistic theology and liturgical practice (the frequency of reception of the Eucharist, the forms of distribution, the preparation and shape of the bread) must suffice.[15] They also link with the question raised in the first section.

As a transition to the final section, one further aspect should at least be touched on in our historical survey. Consensus and dissent in questions of faith leaves a trace in liturgical prayer in that one prays for the churches with which one is in communion. In practice, that means that the names of their bishops are mentioned in the eucharistic prayer. The personal heads stand for the churches to whose faith they bear witness. If consensus turns into dissent, the names are struck out of the diptychs, and the record of community in faith and love enshrined in the liturgical prayer is cancelled.[16]

III. Consensus and Ordinations

At an early date, Justin described the role of the community in the liturgical celebration by saying "All the people present assent by saying *Amen*"; and by the time of Hippolytus at the latest the acclamation *Dignum et iustum est* had become a fixed part of the ritual.[17] There has been no change since in this liturgical expression of the community's role, and a German saying may be quoted as evidence: "As sure as the Amen in the Church." Does this imply discrimination against the community? Surely we must accept that the celebration of the liturgy is not,

---

[15] See J. A. Jungmann, *Missarum Sollemnia* I (Freiburg, ⁵1952), pp. 98–122; also J. R. Geiselmann, *Die Abendmahlslehre an der Wende der christlichen Spätantike zum Frühmittelalter* (Munich, 1933).

[16] See O. Stegmüller, "Diptychon", *Reallexikon für Antike und Christentum* III (1957), pp. 1138–49.

[17] See Th. Klauser, "Akklamation", *Reallexikon f. Antike u. Christentum* I (1950), pp. 216–33.

in theory at least, the place where the community is given a chance to distance itself from its officers and make known its dissent. The liturgical assembly is of its nature the area in which agreement in faith and love is expressed.

If that is true, one must ask whether the community has any opportunity at all to express its *sensus*. It had once, at least. The history of the liturgy of ordination tells us of "the people of God's right of election".[18] In the early period of the Church, agreement and dissent were expressed directly,[19] but from the Middle Ages onwards, as the Roman and—following Roman practice—the Frankish liturgical books indicate, the right to a say seems to have been restricted to the right to bring objections against the candidates' conduct.[20] None the less, Frankish liturgical texts show that in the eighth century the community was still asked for its agreement to the candidacies.[21] Even if the fact that, according to the evidence of the liturgical books, this agreement was not sought before the day of ordination itself, but within the liturgy of ordination, shows how far liturgical language and the legal practice of the day had diverged, the words addressed to the community are still worth noting: "We remember how our fathers wisely ordained that in the choice of those who were to serve at the altar the people also should be consulted."[22]

I do not need to trace the participation of the community in the choice of their ministers any further. Until very recently the ordination liturgies kept the old texts, with their evidence of

---

[18] See B. Kleinheyer, *Die Priesterweihe im römischen Ritus. Eine liturgiehistorische Studie* (Trier, 1962), and R. Kottje and H. Th. Risse, *Wahlrecht für das Gottesvolk? Erwägungen zur Bischofs- und Pfarrerwahl* (Düsseldorf, 1969).

[19] Kleinheyer, *op. cit.*, pp. 22-4.

[20] Kleinheyer, *op. cit.*, pp. 49-52.

[21] *Missale Francorum*, 21 (Mohlberg, 6) on ordination to the diaconate: "*an eum dignum hoc officio censeatis, scire desidero*"; *ibid.*, 35 (Mohlberg, 10 f.) for the consecration of a bishop: "*Virum venerabilem illum testimonio persbyterorum et totius cleri et consilio civium et consistentium credimus eligendum. . . . Hunc ergo, dilectissimi fratres, testimonii boni operis electum, dignissimum sacerdotium laudibus clamate et dicite: Dignus est.*"

[22] *Ibid.*, 27 (Mohlberg 8) from the ordination of priests; see Kleinheyer, *op. cit.*, pp. 95-6.

former active participation in the selection of candidates.[23] In the reform of the liturgy of ordination,[24] the tradition has been developed further, and the elements of the choice of candidates have been given a form that corresponds to the present legal position and is open to new developments that may give back to the communities an opportunity to express their consent.

Candidates for ordination to the priesthood are asked: "Are you prepared to celebrate the mysteries of Christ in faith and reverence, in accordance with the tradition of the Church, to the praise of God and the salvation of his people? Are you prepared to serve the word of God in the knowledge of the responsibility you bear when you preach the Good News and teach the Catholic faith?"[25] Similarly, at the ordination of a bishop the candidate is required to declare before the community that he is prepared to preserve the faith pure and whole, as handed down by the apostles and always and everywhere preserved in the Church; that he is prepared to care for the people of God with his assistants, the presbyters and deacons, like a good father and lead them on the path of salvation; and that for love of the Lord he is prepared to be kind and compassionate to the poor, the homeless and all those in distress.[26] These are criteria for the selection of ministers which no one can ignore, and which take precedence over any other considerations as to the fitness of a candidate.

When, in the rite for the ordination of a bishop, the representative of the local church comes before the consecrator at the beginning of the ceremony and asks him, in the name of the local church, to ordain the chosen candidate as its bishop,[27] and when, in the rite for the ordination of presbyters and deacons, the answer to the ordaining minister's question whether the candidates are worthy is, "The people and their leaders have been asked, and I

[23] See the rites for the ordination of priests and deacons in the pre-1968 *Pontificale Romanum*.

[24] See B. Kleinheyer, "Weiheliturgie in neuer Gestalt", *Liturgisches Jahrbuch* 18 (1968), pp. 210–29; *id.*, "L'Ordination des prêtres", *La Maison-Dieu* 78 (1969), pp. 95–112; *id.*, "La riforma degli Ordini sacri", *Rivista Liturgica* 56 (1969), pp. 8–24.

[25] *Pontificale Romanum* (1968), "De ordinatione presbyterorum", 15.

[26] *Ibid.*, "De ordinatione episcopi", 19.

[27] *Ibid.*, "De ordinatione episcopi", 16.

declare that they think them worthy",[28] must there really be no more activity in the communities in connection with the choice of candidates than canon law at present provides for? The consent of the community to the prayers of those who are appointed to serve at the altar, which is rightly asked in the liturgical celebration, will have all the more weight if the communities are given greater responsibility in the choice of candidates for offices in the Church.[29]

Translated by Francis McDonagh

[28] *Ibid.*, "De ordinatione presbyterorum", 12.

[29] Balthasar Fischer ends his important essay, "Das Gebet der Kirche als Wesenselement des Weihesakramentes", *Liturgisches Jahrbuch* 20 (1970), pp. 166–77, by quoting the Protestant theologian J. J. von Allmen: "A priest must realize that he has to see his ministry as an answer to the prayer of the Church."

Hervé-Marie Legrand

Theology and the Election of Bishops in the Early Church

I. A Practical or a Theological Problem?

SINCE the conclusion of the Council the dioceses of Western Europe, North America and especially South America have recorded an increasing number of requests from Christians, whether ordained or not, to participate in the choice of their bishop, and even calling for the restoration of the election of the bishop by the local church, as in patristic times.[1] What is the spiritual climate in which requests of this kind come into being? Are they a direct consequence of the ecclesiological reorientation of Vatican II, which gave back to Catholics the sense of being the people of God, and set the ministry in its proper place in the Church?[2] Do others hope in this way to weaken what they consider the excessively burdensome yoke of Rome, which freely appoints the bishops of the whole Church, at least in principle? Are others concerned with a return to patristic sources? Or, more prosaically, in a society with apparently democratic institutions, is there a wish that the Church too should become democratic, not only to make it credible in the eyes of our contemporaries,

---

[1] There have been many initiatives in this direction since 1966: there is a list of the most recent in R. Laurentin, *Nouveaux ministères et fin du clergé* (Paris, 1971), p. 230. Theologians and canon lawyers have also taken the matter up: cf. the special number of *Theological Quarterly* 149 (1969), 2 and W. W. Basset (ed.), *The Choosing of Bishops* (Canon Law Society of America; Hartford, Conn., 1971). See also G. Thils, *Choisir les évêques? Élire le pape?* (Paris-Gembloux, 1970).

[2] Cf. *Lumen Gentium*, and the significant order of chapters 2 and 3.

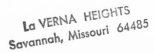

but simply because the same man who is an adult in the world finds it painful to be treated as a child in the Church?

Without detailed research, it is perhaps risky to evaluate the respective influence of each of these factors. If, as is probable, the decisive factor in these requests is the desire for the Church to be more democratic, they will increase until it is very difficult to ignore them. The greater or lesser degree of parallelism which has always existed between patterns of participation in political life and in the life of the Church makes a considerable modification in the present mode of appointing bishops very likely.

The prospect of seeing the local church once again take part in the choosing of its bishop rightly gives rise to many fears and many hopes. A study of them would depend upon one's pastoral viewpoint. Without underestimating the need for such a study, I shall here consider the preliminary and more fundamental question. Is there a solid theological basis for requiring the participation of a church in the choice of its bishop? Or is this an archaic idea of little significance, as the fate of the institution might suggest? For the Church has recognized many other ways of becoming a bishop as legitimate besides the primitive institution providing for the election of the bishop by the whole *ecclesia*: election by the clergy alone or by the chapter alone; or else, a practice which departs even further from election, appointment by the episcopal synod or by the pope alone; and even, throughout the centuries to the present day, by the secular—sometimes non-Catholic—authorities.[3]

These facts raise a question. Is the way of appointing bishops theologically a matter of indifference in itself, and does it depend principally upon historical and sociological criteria, the main one being efficiency? Alternatively, should this mode of appointment be subject to strictly theological criteria, of the same kind as the internal structure of the Church? Before any position is adopted this question must be answered. For is it possible to put an end to these requests if one wished to do so, without refusing them in a theological convincing way? And if one wishes to accede to

---

[3] Thus the czars of Russia appointed the Latin bishops, cf. Phillimore, *International Law*, II, 411. There is a study of the state privileges at present in force in H.-M. Legrand, *La charge pastorale des évêques* (Paris, 1969), pp. 148-63.

them, is there not a danger in doing so without having made explicit in theological terms the various reasons that motivate them? Thus a theological debate is both necessary and inevitable.

This article is intended to contribute to the debate by expounding the profound ecclesiological significance of the canonical and liturgical institutions of the election-ordination of bishops in the early Church. There is no intention of conferring on the early period a privileged status which is not justified by chronology alone, far less of suggesting that fidelity to tradition requires imitation. The intention is simply to restore the significance of what our fathers in the faith did.

However limited this approach, it will reveal a meaning which by its very richness cannot but be a challenge to our present practice. And this challenge may well prove to be made in the name and of the true tradition, which we betray all the more casually in that we have forgotten it.

II. Is Election the Norm for the Appointment of Bishops?

1. *Election by the Local Church*

Until 1917, election remained the norm of the written law for the appointment of bishops in the Catholic Church. In this respect, the present can. 329 represents a considerable innovation in its statement that "the Bishop of Rome freely appoints them (i.e., bishops)" (§2), and especially when it specifies (§3) that if a chapter or any moral person retains the right of election this is by virtue of a *concession*. This is the first time in history that such a statement appeared in a legislative text, at least in such categorical and general terms. Hence the untrammelled right of the pope to appoint any bishop is not traditional. In the course of two thousand years of history, even if the letter of the law was often twisted, the norm professed by the Church was that of election. Is this continuity of written law without significance? I cannot here summarize the history of elections, which is a familiar one. It is attested in the *Didache*. Towards 230, the *Apostolic Tradition* of Hippolytus clearly lays down the principle: "Let him be ordained as bishop who has been chosen by all the people ... by the consent of all, let the bishops lay their hands upon him", a principle which St Cyprian considers as of divine right.[4] In order not to multiply examples, let us give as typical the recommendations of two popes of the middle of the fifth century, both of whom were in other respects very conscious of the prerogatives of their see. St Celestine states: "Let a bishop not be imposed upon the people whom they do not want."[5] St Leo is even more explicit: "He who has to preside over all must be elected by all", or again, "Let a person not be ordained against the wish of the Christians and whom they have not explicitly asked for."[6] We can see that in the early period, when the Christian community was free to organize its own life itself, it insisted upon respect for the practice of election, through the mouthpiece of its bishops and popes, who are also saints. How was this norm first breached? How did it fall into disuse? It is essential to note that this evolution is the result of external and secular pressure and not of a more profound doctrinal view.

2. Elections not Abandoned for Theological Reasons

The progressive decay of ancient institutions is explained both in the East and in the West by the constant pressure of the political authorities. In order to resist them more effectively, in the thirteenth century the Church in the West restricted election to the clergy, not without causing an imbalance within the institution.

When, at the beginning of the sixteenth century, Rome granted Catholic monarchies the right of appointment to those sees which had been reserved to Rome itself (for financial reasons) in the Avignon period, the reason was that this right represented ready money and was the most powerful political lever it possessed. Not until the twentieth-century was the Holy See able to take advantage of the secularization of Catholic states, and win back for the Church the free right to appoint bishops. This right was reserved to the Holy See in the movement towards centralization which followed Vatican I.

The development I have summarized gives no grounds for suspicion on doctrinal grounds of the election of bishops.[7] This

[4] *Epist.* 67, 4.   [5] *Epist.* 4, 5 (PL 50, col. 434).
[6] *Ad Anast.* (PL 54, col. 634).
[7] The election of bishops is still to some extent in favour with Rome,

was something which it is necessary to establish before turning to examine the profound meaning of elections.

III. THE STRUCTURE OF THE ELECTION-ORDINATION OF BISHOPS IN THE EARLY CHURCH

I use the term "election-ordination" to describe the way a bishop was created in the early Church, since a single liturgical act united organically his election by the people (including the clergy), the laying on of hands by the bishops (order) and his entry into office (jurisdiction): at that time an ordination without election and without office was as unthinkable as a jurisdiction without order.[8] The organic nature of the liturgical act can be seen in the various ways in which the local church (*a*), the neighbouring bishops (*b*), the elected bishop himself (*c*) and, outside any set framework and present at every moment, the principal agent, the Holy Spirit (*d*), are all involved in it.

1. *The Part played by the Local Church*

Significantly, a bishop at the present day is often ordained outside his diocese. For our fathers in the faith, this would have been senseless, so vital and inalienable was the role of the local church. It was concerned as much as the bishop. To sum up:

(*a*) *It called the bishop*: In concrete terms, his vocation is his election by the brotherhood of Christians: "as before the judgment of God and Christ, in the presence of the Holy Spirit" (*Apostolic Constitutions VIII*). This is so true that the elected person was often ordained unwillingly and under constraint (*invitus, coactus*). The election of the greatest bishops of antiquity

---

since, having had the opportunity of abolishing it on the occasion of several concordats, did not do so. Cf. R. Metz, "La choix des évêques dans les récents concordats (1918–1954)", *L'Année canonique* 3 (1954/5), pp. 74–98.

[8] The main texts are given by L. Mortari, *Consacrazione episcopale e collegialità* (Florence, 1969; preface by H. von Campenhausen). H. Dombois' interpretations in *Das Recht der Gnade* (Witten, 1961), chapters 9 and 13.2, are interesting.

(Ambrose, Augustine, Martin of Tours, Gregory the Great, Basil, etc.) shows that this is much more than a literary conceit.[9]

(b) *The local church could check that the bishop-elect held the apostolic faith, and bore witness to this fact.* This was the meaning of the scrutiny, to which all rites bear witness, or of the profession of faith before the congregation. The witness which the people bear to the faith of the elected bishop can clearly be seen in the description of *Apostolic Constitutions VIII.* Here is something which casts light on the apostolicity required of the Church. All Christians are responsible for it, especially when one of them enters the apostolic ministry. This is not to deny the functional and specific responsibility of the clergy, but makes it impossible to represent the apostolicity of the Church as if it were a consequence solely of the apostolicity of the ministry. Rather, the latter is an expression of the apostolicity of the whole Church, and a specific responsibility with regard to it.

(c) *The local church carries out an action of reception with regard to the bishop, having played a part in giving him to itself.* To say that the local church *gave itself* its bishop would be to misinterpret the practice of early Christians. The consent of the church in the election was regarded as a gift of the Spirit, and once the bishop had been elected and ordained, he was received by the church as one designated by the Spirit.

2. *The Part played by the Neighbouring Bishops*

After Nicaea (can. 4), which reaffirms an older practice, the presence of three bishops at least is required for an episcopal ordination. They are not there to make the ceremony dignified, nor to guarantee the validity of the ordination, as modern writers have said, nor to exercise the powers of the episcopal college upon this particular church. Three expressions will serve to define their role as representatives of their churches: witness, tradition-reception and the laying on of hands within the framework of the epiclesis of the whole assembly.

(a) *The bishops are witnesses.* No church can be sure of its

---

[9] Cf. Y. Congar, "Ordinations invitus, coactus de l'Eglise au canon 214", *Rev. Sc. Phil. Theol.* 50 (1966), pp. 169–97.

apostolicity if this is not attested by others. By their presence and their action, the neighbouring bishops bear witness to the identity in matters of faith and apostolic ministry of the church, celebrating the ordination with the apostolic Church throughout space and time.

(b) *The action of the bishops: transmission and reception.* In laying their hands on the newly elected bishop, the bishops constitute him as an unimpeachable and personal witness of the apostolic faith, in his function as a link and as president of the church. In this sense, they *transmit* the apostolic ministry to him. At the same time they *receive him* as the representative of his church to other churches. In this way he becomes a member of the college of bishops, not in the sense of a ruling group of the universal Church, but in the sense of the responsibility of all the churches in communion.

(c) *The bishops are ministers of the gift of the Spirit in the setting of the epiclesis of the whole assembly.* In ordination the newly elected bishop receives a charisma which the rituals call *pneuma higemonikon, spiritus principalis,* that is, a gift for the leadership of the community. This gift is not transmitted by those who carry out the ordination, but by God himself, who responds to the epiclesis of the whole assembly. For the *ecclesia* gathered together is the integral subject carrying out the celebration, as it is of every liturgical action.

3. *The Bishop-Elect*

The very structure of the election-ordination clearly reveals its intention, which is above all an ecclesiological one. By this act the new bishop both becomes the real representative of his church to others, and receives the task of representing the whole Church in his own church: he is the principal instrument of the conciliarity of the Church. Both aspects of his mediatory office must be taken into account. For otherwise there is a risk of restricting him to his local church, and treating his concern for the whole Church as optional; or alternatively, of making him a member of an organ of authority over and above the church, and so uprooting him from his own concrete church.

4. *The Holy Spirit, the Principal Agent in the Ordination*

Modern writers have a tendency to restrict the action of the Spirit solely to the laying on of hands by the bishops. In reality, the Spirit is active at every moment in election-ordination. He is there in the vocation-election, conceived of as a judgment by God and not as a democratic election in which everyone votes according to his interest or free choice. He comes in response to the epiclesis; he is at the basis of the reception as he was of the bishop-elect's testimony of faith.

The fundamentally charismatic structure of the Church is displayed in this manifold action of the Spirit in the election-ordination. In this light it is possible to overcome the false opposition between function and charisma, which gives the worst of both worlds: ordained Christians dismiss charismata as exceptional, while "charismatics" believe they have no need to respect the order of ministries established in the Spirit. Again, one can see how all Christians are equal within the variety established by the Spirit, and why a hierarchical understanding of the ordained ministry is inadequate. Finally, one can see how little basis there is for the christological short-circuit by which ordained ministers trade on their title of ministers of Christ to withdraw themselves from their community and especially to reserve to themselves the monopoly of choosing other ministers; whereas in fact no one is a minister of Christ without being a minister of the Church.

IV. THE ORIGINALITY OF THE MUTUAL INCLUSION OF THE BISHOPS AND THEIR CHURCH

1. *The Originality of the Election-Ordination as an Institution*

Some people have reduced Christian ordination to a simple rite of installation or entry into office. At the period we are examining, it was radically different from this. Unlike the magistrate or officials of the time, a bishop did not become a bishop by making the first act of his office. Moreover, ordination was not identical simply with election by the local church: the reception and the laying on of hands by the representatives of the neighbouring churches was required. There is no known parallel to such an institution, and it integrated the bishop with the church in an original way.

2. *"The Bishop is in the Church and the Church is in the Bishop"* (*St Cyprian*)

The law of election-ordination bears clear witness to the inclusion of the bishop within the church. The canons forbade him to pass on his office himself: the right of appointment reverted to the church. More important, for the canon law of the same period the consent of a church to the ordination of its bishop was always required, whereas the person to be ordained might be validly ordained under constraint. The church had to consent to the bishop, and not the reverse. There was never an appeal to the Christian obedience of the people to retain an undesirable bishop (*nullus invitis detur episcopus!*). On the contrary, until 1917, under the heading of *malitia plebis* (the wickedness of the people!) the law lays down that such a bishop has an obligation to resign. The *Codex* of 1917 maintains this obligation only for parish priests (can. 2147 2, 2). Thus by his ordination the bishop does not cease to be a brother. Yet the understanding of the ordination as a transmission recalls that the ministry does not derive from the local community and that in this respect the bishop can be distinguished from it. And this is of great value to the church, for by this it knows that it is not gathered together in its own name.

Finally, the inclusion of the bishop in the church is a very original conception. But the well-known formula of St Cyprian, if understood dynamically, gives expression to an inclusion which in some respects is reciprocal: "The bishop is in the church and the church in the bishop." This shows how little justice is done to reality by strongly contrasted categories such as those of the teaching Church and the learning Church, and the like. It also means that ordinations of bishops without a concrete church are meaningless. There is no justification for them in the doctrine of collegiality.

V. THE ELECTION OF BISHOPS BY THEIR CHURCH: A COMPLEX THEOLOGICAL REQUIREMENT

Analysis of the very original procedure of election-ordination reveals an organic ecclesiology in which the participation of a

church in the choice of its bishop is seen to be a structural requirement. This participation is not a venerable custom, one among
other equally legitimate customs. To take away this stone from
the edifice of authentically Catholic and traditional ecclesiology
is to cause it to totter. When an original institution is supplanted
by an administrative centralization, an ecclesiology of communion is no longer being operated, neither between churches
nor at the heart of the local church. This reduction of the local
church to a state of passivity has harmful effects.

(a) When the aspect of communion in ordination (witness,
reception) is obliterated, the emphasis is then on its consecratory
aspect. There is a risk here of giving too much weight to the
aspect of transmission at the expense of the aspect of communion.

(b) In the same way, the link between the apostolicity of the
whole Church and that of its ministers is obliterated, and there is
a risk that the person who witnesses is regarded as more important than the witness he bears.

(c) The structure of the Church as a brotherhood is no longer
expressed.

(d) Finally, if the diocese is regarded as a sub-division of the
universal Church, the original relationship between the local
church and the universal Church is altered. Ultimately, all this
betrays a general weakness in pneumatology. Christomonism
dominates the theology of the ministries more seriously than any
other. It can be seen that the participation of churches in the
choice of their bishops is a profoundly Catholic requirement, if
the word "Catholic" is to mean plenitude, balance and respect
for tradition.

Some False Trails to be Avoided

(a) *The "democratic" misunderstanding.* A mechanical restoration of elections, with universal suffrage on the democratic
pattern, would lead to theological confusion. Of course the bishop
is the representative of his electors, but he is also the representative of the whole Church to them. Moreover, he does not receive
his commission from them, but from the Spirit, in a college going
back to the apostles of the Lord. Finally, the reciprocity which
exists between him and the church is not one of contract, but is

based upon a confession of faith which cannot be judged by majority vote. In spirit and in structure, the election-ordination of a bishop is something different from liberal democracy.[10]

(b) *The false trail of competition with the papal primacy.* According to *Lumen Gentium* 22, the relationship between the pope and the bishops reproduces that which existed between Peter and the other apostles: they were chosen without any intervention on his part. The direct nomination of virtually all Catholic bishops by the pope does not derive from his primacy, but from historical circumstances which allowed the pope to remove it from the hands of the civil authorities. In dogmatic terms, there is nothing to prevent and everything to recommend the pope's returning, in suitable pastoral conditions, to the policy of St Leo: "That no one should be ordained bishop against the wish of the Christians and whom they have not explicitly asked for." "He who has to preside over all must be elected by all." For according to Vatican I itself, the instruction and guidance of the episcopate is one of the tasks of the papal primacy,[11] but if the Holy See feels that there is an attempt to make elections a weapon against the papal primacy, the whole affair will be diverted along a false trail. This would be so in spite of the ecclesiological anomaly of the present situation and its serious ecumenical disadvantages with regard to Orthodoxy.

(c) *The false trail of elections by ordained Christians only.* In the Eastern Catholic churches, the synod elects the bishops, as the chapter of canons does in about twenty Western dioceses. It is no solution to make this procedure a general one. When the clergy co-opt within their own closed circle, this is not yet the church participating in the choice of its bishop. That would be realized in concrete terms if for example all Christians could make suggestions, and the pastoral council of the diocese (including members of the *presbyterium* and elected laymen) conducted an election which had to be approved by the episcopal conference, the pope having to receive the newly elected bishop

---

[10] This is not to prejudge the meaning to be given to the "democratization of the Church".

[11] Cf. the words, to which little attention has been paid, of *Pastor Aeternus*, which quote Gregory the Great in this sense, Denz. *Ench.* 3061.

into his communion.[12] This would be perhaps the most faithful translation of the ancient ecclesiology of communion which is trying to come back to life.

Here I do not look at the matter from the pastoral point of view. A political analysis would be needed for that. This study has a different aim: to give a clear outline of the theology of the election of bishops. But I must emphasize that the designation of the person of the bishop is less important than the way in which his office functions. It would be sad to forget that there is a possibility for the Church, here and now, to stop being an institution massively dependent upon the clergy and to become the concern of all Christians—a communion.

Translated by R. A. Wilson

---

[12] Already, in the present law, the pope does not confirm the election of the Catholic patriarchs, cf. for the election of Maximos V (Melkite): "The new patriarch communicated to the Holy See the news of his election, and the pope, instead of a confirmation pure and simple, notified him that he had been received into ecclesiastical communion". *Irénikon* 40 (1967), p. 565.

Yves Congar

Reception as an Ecclesiological Reality

EVEN if this is not a dangerous theme, it is one that is not often examined. This is strange, for it is of major importance from the viewpoint of ecumenism as from that of a wholly traditional and Catholic ecclesiology.[1]

[1] The following is a list of studies to which I refer hereafter by the appropriate letter, together with the page number. An extended text of the present article, with more detailed notes, is to be found in fasc. 3 of the *Revue des Sciences philosophiques et théologiques*, 1972. (A) R. Sohm, *Kirchenrecht*, I (Leipzig, 1892), pp. 320, 322-44; II (Munich & Leipzig, 1923), p. 71. (B) J. Haring, "Die ehre von der Epikie. Eine rechtwissenschaftliche Studie", *Theol. Quartalschr.*, 52 (1899), pp. 576-600, 796-810. (C) J. Didiot, art. "Acceptation des lois", *Dict. théol. Cath.*, I/1 (1903), col. 295-9 (wholly negative). (D) L. de Duca, "L'accettazione popolare della legge canonica nel pensiero di Graziano e de suoi interpreti", *Studia Gratiana*, vol. III (Bologna, 1955), pp. 193-276. (E) Y. Congar, "Quod omnes tangit ab omnibus tractari et approbari debet", *Rev. hist. droit français et etr.*, 36 (1958), pp. 210-59. (F) E. W. Kemp, *Counsel and Consent. Aspects of the government of the Church as exemplified in the history of the English provincial synods* (London, 1961). (G) Peter Fransen, "L'autorité des conciles", in "Problèmes de l'autorité (*Unam Sanctam*, 58) (Paris, 1962), pp. 59-100. (H) Livin Stan, "The 'reception' by the Church of ecumenical decisions" (in Rumanian), in *Studii Theologice*, ser. II, XVII, no. 7-8 (Sept.-Oct., 1965), pp. 395 ff.; "Uber die Rezeption der Beschlusse der oekumenischen Synoden seitens der Kirche", in *Theologia* (Athens), 40 (1969), pp. 158-68. (I) *Councils and the Ecumenical Movement* (World Council Studies, 5) (Geneva, 1968). Articles by Greenslade and Käppers. (J) *The Ecumenical Review*, 22 October 1970): "The Reception of the Council of Chalcedon by the Churches". Mesrob Ashjian, "The Acceptance of the Ecumenical Councils by the Armenian Church, with special reference to the Council of Chalcedon", pp. 348-62; J. Coman, "The Doctrinal Definitions of the Council of Chalcedon and its Reception in

The very term "reception" has been used in modern times by legal historians, mainly Germans, in regard to the part played by Roman law in the usage of ecclesiastical or civil society, as in Germany from the fifteenth century. Grillmeier, who produced a major study of the Council and reception (L) drew on a recent analysis by one of these legal historians, F. Wieacker (*Privatrechtsgeschichte der Neuzeit*, 2nd ed., Göttingen, 1967). Wieacker is of the opinion that reception does not exist in the strict sense unless two different cultural areas are involved, one of which takes over a law pertaining to the other: in the strict sense of the word, reception is "exogenous". Grillmeier has made an interesting attempt to avoid a too global treatment of the reception of Councils, as formulated by Sohm within a stimulating though questionable systematic framework. Grillmeier tries to apply Wieacker's principle—a *genuine* reception is exogenous. Accordingly, reception would exist properly only in the case of the reception of specific synods by the universal Church or by a very large part of the Church, or by separate Churches: for example, if the Nestorians were to accept Ephesus, or the Monophysites Chalcedon. Anything else is reception in a wider, imprecise sense.

This way of looking at reception seems too narrow. Of course there must always be a certain distance, a certain difference, between the party which gives and that which receives. But if one remains within the framework of the one Church, its nature or its firm requirement of communion prevents the difference from being total. It is true that the theme of reception may have an ecumenical interest: there is a concern for reception within the framework of the ecumenical Council of Churches, for example in regard to the re-establishment of communion between the pre-Chalcedonics and the Orthodox (or the Catholics) (cf. H, I and J): this is a sign that a new chapter is beginning in this regard. But history offers an enormous array of actual "receptions", and

the Orthodox Church of the East", pp. 363–82; A. Grillmeier, "The Reception of Chalcedon in the Roman Catholic Church", pp. 383–411; E. R. Hardy, "Chalcedon in the Anglican Tradition", pp. 412–23. (K) R. Dombois, *Das Recht der Gnade. Oekumenisches Kirchenrecht* (Witten, 1961), pp. 825–36. (L) A. Grillmeier, "Konzil und Rezeption. Methodische Bemerkungen zu einem Thema der ökumenischen Diskussion", *Theologie u. Philosophie*, 45 (1970), pp. 321–52.

theories of reception within the one Church. I want to explain the ecclesiological value of this fact. By "reception", I understand (in the present article) the process by means of which a church (body) truly takes over as its own a resolution that it did not originate in regard to its self, and acknowledges the measure it promulgates as a rule applicable to its own life. Reception includes something more than what the Scholastics called "obedience". For the Scholastics it is the act by which a subordinate submits his will and conduct to the legitimate precepts of a superior, out of respect for the latter's authority. Reception is not a mere realization of the relation "secundum sub et supra": it includes a degree of consent, and possibly of judgment, in which the life of a body is expressed which brings into play its own, original spiritual resources.

I. The Facts

That the concept of reception is still valid was shown adequately by Vatican II in its envisaging a collegial initiative emanating from the bishops, which could be a "verus actus colegialis" only if the pope approved it "vel libere recipiat".[2] This text speaks of the reception of the privilege of the bishop of Rome that Vatican II so firmly reaffirmed and to which history bears adequate witness. It constitutes an authentic statement regarding reception since it is a matter of consent (by means of judgment) by one church body to a resolution put forward by others. Apart from this, law as at present knows no case of reception (so far as I am aware) other than acceptance by the pope, and, after him, by the world episcopate, of new bishops of the Eastern rite elected to their patriarchate after a mere "nihil obstat" from Rome, but neither named nor confirmed by the Holy See. The word "reception" was not pronounced, but its essence inhered in the expressions "recognize in its communion", "put its trust in and adhere to the free decisions of the Patriarchs and their synods".[3]

---

[2] *Lumen Gentium,* 22 end; *Christus Dominus,* 4; in the 1970 version of the *Lex Ecclesiae fundamentalis,* can. 41 and 46, 1.

[3] Communication from the Cardinal president of the Central Commission for the Co-ordination of Post-conciliar work and Interpretation of decrees of the Council, dated 24 May 1966, and a letter from the Eastern Congregation to Patriarch Maximos IV, dated 22 June 1966.

It is not in the present *ius conditum* that we can find anything substantial on reception. The actual life of the Church should prove more instructive. But it is history that we must interrogate for positive information.

(*a*) *The Councils.* The creed of Nicaea was "received" *in toto* only after fifty-six years of contentions punctuated by synods, excommunications, exiles, and imperial interventions and violence. The synods of Tyr and Jerusalem, in 335, deposed Athanasius and rehabilitated Arius. Pope Julius himself would not seem always to have been of the opinion that the judgment of Nicaea was irrevocably established. The Council of Constantinople of 381 marked the end of these quarrels. And that very Council owes its designation as ecumenical not to its composition (which was not at all ecumenical: St Ambrose complained that Rome and the West were ignored and absent—Epist. 14. 4–8; PL 16, 952–3) but solely to the reception of its creed by the Council of Chalcedon as the most proficient expression of the faith of Nicaea. In fact the so-called Chalcedonian creed was read after the Nicene creed, and the canons of 381 were taken as "synodikon of the second Council". But it was only in 519, and at first more by tacit acquiescence that Rome, or rather Pope Hormisdas, in "receiving" the profession of faith of Patriarch John, recognized Constantinople as second of the first four Councils.[4] The history of the third Council was hardly such as to allow it to be considered as properly ecumenical. A decision was rushed through by Cyril of Alexandria before the arrival of the Syrian bishops four days later, and that of the legates eighteen days later; and there were two assemblies (without any contacts between them). It was only because of the agreement reached during the two subsequent years between Cyril and his group, and John of Antioch and his supporters, that Ephesus was able to reach an elementary state of ecumenism. Newman often argued from this historic episode to the usage of those for whom the opposition of

[4] Cf. A. M. Ritter, *Das Konzil von Konstantinopel und sein Symbol* (Forschg. z. Kirchen- und Dogmengesch. 15) (Göttingen, 1965). T. Camelot says in this regard: "It is a kind of consensus of the Church after the event that has recognized this (ecumenical) character of a Council which was ecumenical neither in intention nor in actuality" ("Les conciles oecuméninques des IVe et Ve siècles", in *Le Concile et les conciles* (Chevetogne & Paris, 1960), p. 73.

a large minority (during the First Vatican Council until the definition of 18 July 1871 inclusively) constituted a decisive barrier. The subsequent accession of those on the other side, that is their "reception", was like a "complement to the Council and an integral part of it".

With the creeds of Nicaea and Constantinople, Chalcedon had also "received" the works of St Leo and the two letters of St Cyril (second session).[5] The famous "Peter has spoken through the mouth of Leo", exactly like the "Peter has spoken by the mouth of Agathon" of the sixth ecumenical Council against Monothelitism (as anathematized by Pope Honorius), was an act of reception: the Council recognizes Peter's declaration of faith in the pope's formulary. But the total and definitive reception of Chalcedon itself required many explanations: it was a long story (cf. J: Coman and Grillmeier). There was non-reception, at least legally and literally, either from the Armenian hierarchy, or the Egyptian Copts, because of anti-Nestorianism: reaction, in the one case against Persia, and in the other against Byzantium, in terms of rejection of an "exogenous" decision. "That abominable council of Chalcedon", said John Rufus, Bishop of Maïouna around A.D. 515 (J, p. 371), just as some integrists now talk of "that awful Second Vatican Council...".

On the other hand, "reception" was sometimes established and expressed by means of explicit decisions. In this respect, acceptance by the apostolic Holy See of Rome was decisive in the West (cf. J, pp. 387-9). But reception was also confirmed by means of a more extended and complex process employing proclamation (the kerygmatic aspect), spirituality and theological elaboration (see J: Coman and Grillmeier). The liturgy consecrated and definitively assured the trinitarian and christological doctrines: *lex orandi*.

It is possible to study the history of all the Councils from the angle of their reception. The last that we had in common with the Orthodox East, the second Nicaean Council, of 787, itself proclaimed that for a Council to be considered ecumenical, it had to be received by the *praesules ecclesiarum*, and primarily by the

---

[5] See W. de Vries, "Die Struktur der Kirche gemäss dem Konzil von Chalkedon (431)", *Orient. christ. period.*, 35 (1969), pp. 63-122.

pope.⁶ But this very Council had to wait a long time before it was accepted in the West: not only by the Frankish theologians of the Council of Frankfurt of 794, under the influence of a bad translation and rivalry towards another Empire, but by the papacy, maimed and under attack from the Byzantine Caesaro-papism that seduced into its realm of obedience Sicily, Calabria and Illyria. Not until the profession of faith sent by Leo IX to Peter of Antioch in 1053, was there any *express* reception of Nicaea II by the popes.⁷

I should like to cite a few examples from the West in the second millennium. The Fourth Lateran Council (1215) was received in the West in such a way as permanently to affect the life of the Church: whether because its profession of faith *Firmiter*, reproduced at the head of the Decretals, became a fourth creed and a kind of syllabus of instruction for clergy and faithful, or because sixty of its texts and fifty-nine of its seventy canons entered into ecclesiastical law and then into the Codex of 1917.⁸ In this regard, the reception of a Council is identical with its effectiveness; this point has a certain value, as will become clear, in respect of a theological interpretation of reception. The case of the Council of Trent will serve to illustrate the same remark. In addition, the problem and the difficulty of its "reception" by Protestants recurred incessantly in the correspondence between Leibniz and Bossuet. This was already a case of that "exogenous" reception looked for today in the ecumenical movement in order to bring about a consensus between separated ecclesiastical bodies.

The acceptance of the dogma of 18 July 1870 by the minority bishops who had left Rome the day before in order to avoid pronouncing a "non placet" when the voting was clear, was also a

⁶ In regard to the iconoclastic Council of 753 (which called itself the "seventh ecumenical Council": Mansi 13, 350E), "quam neque receperunt neque concordaverunt reliquarum praesules ecclesiarum": Mansi 13, 208 DE-209 A (Greek), 207 DE–210 A (Latin).

⁷ PL 143, 772 D–773 A. After having declared that he "received and venerated" the first four Councils, Leo IX added: "Pari modo recipio et veneror reliqua tria concilia ..., etc."

⁸ R. Metz, "Les conciles oecuméniques et le Code de droit canonique de 1917", *Rev. de Droit. canon.* 10 (1960), pp. 192–213; R. Foreville, "Lateran I, II, III and Lateran IV" (*Hist. des Conciles oecuméniques* 6) (Paris, 1965), pp. 311–17.

case of reception, and all the more interesting a one inasmuch as many of them, faithful to their principles, grounded this acceptance on the fact that the dogma was "received" by the whole Catholic Church. This was the argument of Mgr Maret. But it was not a convincing argument for Döllinger.

Within the framework of present christological research, which is concerned more with the man-Jesus of the synoptic gospels, there has been talk of the "re-reception" of Chalcedon.[9] Chalcedon was accepted and not contested. But within a new context of christological vision, and of ecumenical inquiry, a new reading of its history and of its underlying intentions is necessary in order to "receive" it once again. It is possible, analogously, to speak of a "re-reception" of Vatican I by Vatican II and, again, in a new context and by means of a renewed reading such as that which allowed the minority of Vatican I to be represented as the *avant-garde* of Vatican II.

I shall now attend to a few literary expressions of this method of reception:

St Augustine enunciates a general principle: "Vides in hac re quid Ecclesiae catholicae valeat auctoritas, quae ab ipsis fundatissimis sedibus apostolorum usque ad hodiernum diem succedentium sibimet episcoporum serie *et tot populorum consensione firmatur* (C. Faust. XI, 1; PL, 42, 246): "In fiducia securae vocis asserer, quod in gubernatione Domini Dei nostri et salvatoris Jesu Christi *universalis Ecclesiae consensione* roboratum est" (De bap. VII, 53: PL 43, 243).

St Leo, speaking of the conciliar canons regarding the right of metropolitans used a formula which was often taken up later: "secundum sanctorum patrum canones Spiritu Dei conditos *et totius mundi reverentia consecratos*" (Epist. 14, 2; PL 54, 672; Jaffé-Ewald-Kaltenbrunner 411): a formula incessantly repeated by Hincmar and other authors of the high Middle Ages.[10] In

---

[9] "Le concile de Chalcédoine. Son histoire, sa réception par les Eglises et son actualité", *Irénikon* 44 (1971), pp. 349–66 (p. 361). Report of the commission for "Faith and Constitution" on the colloquium held in 1969 on this subject.

[10] Cf. Hincmar, PL 125, 384 BC, 1038 A; 126, 113 C, 189 A, 190 C, 199 D, 232 A, 509 B, 510 A, 535 D, and PL 124, 890 AB; *De ordine palatii* 4 (MGH Capit. II, 519); Paschase Radbert, *Vita Walae* II, 16 (PL 120, 1635 A);

regard to the Council of Chalcedon, St Leo wrote: "quae an universis Romani orbis provinciis cum totius mundi est celebrata consensu" (Epist. 164, 3; PL 54, 1150), but what is in question is certainly the internal *consensus* of the Council.

It was another pope, St Simplicius, who held definitively: so "quod apostolicis manibus *cum Ecclesiae universalis assensu . . .*" (10 January 476: Denzinger, 160, not in DSch). St Gelasius, writing in 495 to the bishops of Dardania, gives the criteria which allow a good to be distinguished from a bad Council: The first is that *"quod universalis Ecclesiae probavit assensus"* and that the Holy See approves and holds; the second speaks "contra Scripturas sanctas, contra doctrinam patrum, contra ecclesiasticas regulas, *quam tota merito Ecclesia non recepit* et praecipue sedes apostolica non probavit" (Thiel., I; p. 395); a little later, the Council is described as one accordant with Scripture and tradition *"quam cuncta recipit ecclesia,* quam maxime sedes apostolica comprobatur" (p. 400). That part of *De recipiendis et non recipiendis libris* which may be attributed to Gelasius makes considerable use of the vocabulary of reception: "suscipere", "recipere", etc.

In his synodical letter of February 591 to four other patriarchs, Gregory the Great professed a veneration for the first four Councils, and then the fifth, "quia . . . universa sunt consensu constitua" (Mansi, IX, 104; PL 77, 478; MGM Epp. I, p. 36; Jaffé-Ewald-Kaltenbrunner 1092), quoted by Gratian, 15, c. 2—but he possibly refers to the agreement of the conciliar Fathers.

Dionysius the pseudo-Areopagite was the first to introduce the so-called apostolic canons, those of Sardica and of Africa into the first two redactions of his collection, the *Dionysiaca*. But he excluded them from the third redaction, before 523, and grounded his action thus: "quos non admisit universitas" (Thiel. I, p. 986; F. Maasen, *Geschichte d. Quellen*, I, p. 965).

In his *Pro Defensione trium Capitulorum*, in about 548, Facundus of Hermiane argued insistently for reception by the universal

---

Gerbert, *Ep. ad archiepisc. Senon* (PL 139, 268 B). The theme and the expression were to recur for some time; St Leo's text was cited in the canonical collections: *Anselmo dedicata* I, 105 (104); Yves de Chartres, *Décret* V, 346; Collect. duodec. P.I. 29; Gratian C. XXV, c. 5 (Friedberg, 1013).

Church of the Council of Chalcedon: "in Ecclesia Dei recepta est", "ab Ecclesia universali receptis".[11]

Hincmar of Rheims put forward a fine ecclesiology of the Church as a community, and a theology of the Councils and of reception. He approved of a text of St Leo in this regard. He defined the ecumenical Councils (*generalia*) by the fact that, since they were called by the emperor and consisted of numerous bishops with a "specialis jussia sedis apostolicae" . . . "pro generali ad omnes christianos causa pertinente", they were "a catholica Ecclesia receptissima".[12]

The question of knowing what *constitutes* the ecumenicity of a Council is a complex problem which has been given various answers in the course of history and which is not wholly identical with another question: Who *recognizes* the ecumenicity of a Council? Since Damasius and even since the synod of 368, the popes have affirmed that their approval is necessary, and it is quite certain that no Council can be ecumenical if the see of Rome does not "receive" it. As has been pointed out, Leo and Gelasius united the assent of the whole Church with pontifical approval. But reception by the Church certainly has its place. In the full Council of Trent, Martin Perez de Ayala said, in a treatise composed for the Council: "Est secunda via apprehendendi veritatem in dubiis: Conciliorum scilicet generalium omnium consensione populorum fidelium receptam auctoritem" (*De divinis . . . traditionibus . . . Coloniae*, 1549, pars I, ass. 1; fol. 44ᵛ). It is possible to object to the Slavophile thesis according to which the Councils would have no dogmatic authority by or in themselves, since authority would pertain only to truth, which has no organ other than the Christian mind of the community of the faithful. A considerable number of Orthodox theologians do reject it.[13]

[11] Cf. Lib. II c. 1 and 2 (PL 67, 559 C, 565 B); lib. II c. 1 and 2 (PL 832 D, 834 C, 837 D).

[12] Hincmar, *Opusc. LV, Capit.*, c. 20 (PL 126, 359 AB, 361 A: before June 870). Cf. H. Bacht, "Hinkmar von Reims. Ein Beitrag zur Theologie des allgemeinen Konzils", in *Unio Christianorum, Festgabe L. Jaeger* (Paderborn, 1962), pp. 233-43; *Notre Ecclésiologie du haut moyen-âge* (Paris, 1968), pp. 166-77.

[13] Cf. my note in A. Gratieux, *Le mouvement slavophile à la veille de la Révolution* (*Unam Sanctam*, 25) (Paris, 1953), p. 16 n. 19; B. Schultze,

The texts speak another language. These same theologians, however, retain part of the Slavophile argument: it is not the juridical correction of a Council or its properly formal structure that ensures its authenticity, but the contents of its teaching. In support of this argument, a number of Councils that are just as regular as the others from the formal or juridical point of view, and which were rejected because the Church did not recognize its faith in their decrees, are cited in support of this argument: Rimini-Seleucia, 359, the Council of Ephesus, 449, the iconoclastic synod of Hieria, 753–4, and so on. The Gallicans, who were well acquainted with the history of the Councils, almost to a man held that acceptance by the whole Church was the factor that ultimately allowed recognition of the authority of a Council, its ecumenical character, and the infallibility of its decrees.[14]

On the other hand, many local councils or specific documents acquired a universal value because the Church acknowledged its faith in them, and did so by "reception", by means of a process in which, above all in the West, reception by the see of Rome often played a decisive role. Hence the synod of Antioch in 269 condemned Paul of Samosata; its decision was communicated and received everywhere and proved a serious handicap for Nicaea. Similarly in regard to the anti-Pelagian Council of Carthage of 418 (DSch 222–30): the *Indiculus* written in Rome by Prosper of Aquitaine says, while citing its canons 3, 4 and 5 on grace: "quasi proprium Apostolicae Sedis amplectimur" (DSch 245); yet the *Indiculus* was subsequently incorporated by the pseudo-Dionysius in his collection, which brought about the reception of the Carthaginian canons in the West (cf. M., p. 334). The composite texts of the Council of Orange (Arausio) on grace (DSch, 370–97) were received, even though with some delay (they

"Orthodoxe Kritik an der Ekklesiologie Chomjakovs", *Orient. christ. period.* 36 (1970), pp. 407–31; P. Duprey, "La structure synodale de l'Eglise dans la théologie orientale", *Proche Orient. Chrét.* 20 (1970), pp. 123–45, n. 37.
[14] Cf. W. Palmer, *A Treatise on the Church of Christ*, London, 1838, vol. II, pp. 154 ff.; references: Bossuet, *Lettre à Leibniz* (cf. *infra*); J. B. Bouvier, *Tract. de vera Ecclesia*, p. 234; Mgr de Barral, Archbishop of Tours, *Défense des libertés de l'Eglise gallicane* (Paris, 1817), p. 284; Abbé de Trevern, *Discussion amicale sur l'établissement et la doctrine de l'Eglise anglicane* ... (London, 1816), vol. I, pp. 191 ff. (fifth letter).

RECEPTION AS AN ECCLESIOLOGICAL REALITY   53

were drawn on by the Council of Trent), as possessing an authority which extended beyond the occasion that brought together fourteen bishops at Orange in 529. The same might be said of the credence given the eleventh Council of Toledo in 675, and its trinitarian creed (DSch, 525–41), to the extent that it was "confirmed" by Innocent III, and the Councils of Quierzy (833), Valence (855) on predestination (DSch 621–4 and 625–33). Indeed, it was surely by means of "reception" that the credal article *Quicumque*, of unknown authorship, and the *filioque* were recognized as authentic expressions of faith. In this way, individual Councils, whose actual representation was quite small, came almost, by reception, to rank with general Councils of the Church.

What is essentially important here is what constitutes the authority of Councils and what makes their decisions valid. Some first-class studies are available on this subject.[15] The validity of Councils derives from their expression of the faith of the Apostles and the Fathers, the tradition of the Church (*vide* Athanasius, Cyril of Alexandria and Vincent). The Councils expressed the apostolicity and catholicity of the Church, inasmuch as they represented the totality of the Church and realized a consensus. Athanasius does not appeal to any other principles. After Nicaea (and always taking Nicaea as a model) there was a tendency to stress the assurance that Christ presided over, and the Holy Spirit was present at, Councils of the Church. But the essential thing was to detect in them the faith of the apostles transmitted from the apostolic era by the Fathers of the Church (*Paradosis*). It was certainly for this reason that a Council in ancient times began with a reading of the decrees of previous Councils: it was intended only as a new stage in the process of transmission, but it was also an act of reception.[16] Conciliar theology seems now to

[15] H. Goemans, *Het Algemeen Concilie in de vierde eeuw* (Nijmegen, 1945); my review, *Rev. Sciences phil. théol.* 31 (1947), pp. 288–91; H.-J. Sieben, "Zur Entwicklung der Konzilsidee", *Theologie u. Philosophie* 45 (1970), pp. 353–89; 46 (1971), pp. 40–70, 364–86, 496–528: the first article examines the idea of a general council in Athanasius, the second between Nicaea and Ephesus, the third in St Vincent of Lérins. See also A. S. Greenslade (I).

[16] There is a form of reception of earlier by later Councils: e.g., Chalcedon receives Nicaea and Constantinople, and confirms the ecumenical validity of Ephesus.

be linked with that of apostolicity, of which it is an aspect. Just as the most decisive factor is not the formal succession (*nuda successio*), but the profound identity of the contents and of the faith; just as the two should go together, the most decisive element of a Council is neither the number of participants nor the juridical control of its procedure, but the content of its decisions, even though the two should go together.

If there is a truth universally acclaimed from early times to Vatican II, it is that faith and tradition are borne by the whole Church; that the universal Church is the sole proper subject, under the sovereignty of the Spirit who has been promised to the Church and who dwells in it: "Ecclesia universalis non potest errare". This is why the witness of several neighbouring bishops is required, and indeed that of the community of the faithful, in the case of an election and an ordination. This is why the greatest possible unanimity, agreement and consensus have always been seen as a sign of the action of the Holy Spirit, and therefore a token of truth. A specific theology was able to monopolize the recognition of the ecumenicity of councils and infallibility only by identifying the pope with the Roman church and the Roman church with the universal Church (of which one would not deny the pope was the supreme pastor). It was not by chance that Nicholas I thought of the Roman Church as the "epitome" of the Church, and Pius IX uttered that almost incredible statement: "La Tradizione sono Io!"

*   *   *

Two other cases of reception in essentially doctrinal matters deserve mention:

1. The *canon of Scripture* evolved by a process of reception. The very term is to be found in documents on the subject: the Muratori fragment (lines 66, 72, 82), the decree of the Roman synod of 382 and of Gelasius *De recipiendis et non recipiendis libris*; the decree of 4 February 1441 for the Jacobites "suscipit et veneratur") (DSch 1334), the decree of the Council of Trent on the writings and traditions that are to be received (DSch 1501). This official, normative and express form of reception was preceded by a factual reception in the Churches, as described in the historical works on the subject.

2. The *synodal letters* were a means of communion and unity in the early Church. The Councils sent one to the major centres, such as Rome or Alexandria, in order to communicate their decisions to the other Churches. This fact is particularly well attested in the case of the Councils held before the Constantinian peace in the East or in Africa.[17] Evidently "reception" was the response to this communication. The same is true of the synodal letters and so on that the popes or Eastern patriarchs sent to the major sees, together with their profession of faith, in order to announce their election and to establish communion with them.[18]

(b) *Liturgy*. The extension of certain liturgical forms and unification occurred by means of "receptions" that were in some cases enforced. I shall cite only the reception of the Roman liturgy in the empire of Charlemagne (*Codex Hadrianus* and the Council of Aix, 817); the reception by Rome (then, after and since Rome, by the Latin Church) of the Mainz pontifical in the tenth century, which was of considerable theological significance, and then its ordinal, lent support to the thesis that connected the form of Orders with the "porrectio instrumentorum".[19] It is scarcely possible to use the term "reception" for the way in which Gregory VII substituted the Roman liturgy for the ancient Hispano-Visigothic (or Mozarabic) liturgy in Spain. On the other hand, it can be used for the process by which the Roman liturgy replaced what remained of the "Gallican" rites in France in the nineteenth century.

It is well known that the see of Rome, after Alexander II, then formally and *de jure* from Gregory IX (1234), claimed the sole right to canonize saints. Canonization, which was more a

---

[17] Cf. the letters of the Palestinian Council of c. 190 on the question of Easter (Eusebius, HE V. 23, 2–4); Jerome's (Epist. 33. 4: PL 22, 447) remarks on the "consent" of Rome to the condemnation of Origen by the synods of Alexandria, of 230 and 231; letters from the Council of Carthage of 252 to Cornelius of Rome (cf. St Cyprian, Epist. 41; 42; 55); letter of Cornelius to Fabius of Antioch (Eusebius, HE VII, 30, 1–17); letter from the Council of Arles of 314 to the Pope (Mansi 2, 469–71).

[18] The bishops who elected Maximianus to the see of Constantinople in place of Nestorius, write to Pope Celestine (October 431) and mention this custom as "ecclesiastical".

[19] C. Vogel and R. Elze, "Le Pontifical romano-germanique du 10ᵉ siècle" (*Studi e Testi*, 226, 227) (Vatican, 1963); my *Ecclésiologie du haut moyen-âge* (Paris, 1968), p. 313.

liturgical fact than a juridical decision, had previously been a matter for local churches, and was generalized "accedente totius Ecclesiae consensu et approbatione", as Mabillon says.[20] In this way a decision of the local cult was extended by means of reception. When the popes reserved to themselves the right to canonization, the canonists justified this measure by arguing that only the pope could impose on the whole Church whatever must be held by all. This was the opinion of Innocent and Hostensis. Thomas Aquinas justified with the same argument the reservation to the sovereign pontiff of the promulgation of an article of faith (II^a II^{ae} q. 1, a. 10).

In the same way it is possible to retrace the history of the adoption of liturgical feasts and their diffusion in the West, and, especially in Rome, of a number of Marian feasts celebrated in the East: the Purification, the Nativity, the Presentation, whereas the Immaculate Conception was received progressively from its base in England. ... Just like canonizations, the saints' feasts spread by "reception" before the papacy started to regulate the calendar of what was (improperly) called the "universal Church". The commemoration of the souls of the departed on 2 November, a Cluniac feast established by St Odilo between 1025 and 1030, was introduced into the universal usage of the Latin Church by means of "reception".[21]

(c) *Law and discipline.* The theologians did not wait for the legalists to use the notion of reception. Cf., for example, Nicholas of Cusa, *Concordantia Catholica*, lib. II, cc. 9 and 10 *et seq.* Of course it was mainly the German legal historians who, in the nineteenth century, accredited the term and the concept, in regard to the "reception" of Roman law in Germany from the fifteenth century onwards. But, before that, there was a form "reception" in the Church. This process has been studied age by age. Roman law became an auxiliary form of law, supplying maxims and

[20] *Acta* SS.O.S.B., *Praefatio ad saeculum decimum* (saec. V O.S.B.), VII, 1685, q. LVIII, sectio 6.

[21] I do not know if this formula of the Roman *Martyrology* (1 January) goes back beyond Baronius (1584); the edition of 1914 reads: "Apud Silviniacum, in Gallia, sancti Odilonis, abbatis Cluniacensis, qui primum Commemorationem omnium Fidelium defunctorum, prima die post festum omnium Sanctorum, in suis monasteriis fieri praecepit: *quem ritum postea universalis Ecclesia recipere comprobavit.*"

directives where the canons offered none (Gratian, Lucius III, the decretal *Intelleximus*).[22] As far as I am aware, there has been no adequate and systematic study of the reception or non-reception by the Roman Church of the canons accepted in the East. Hence the Roman Church received only the last thirty-five of the eighty-five so-called apostolic canons accepted in the East, and did not receive the canons of the Quinisext Synod or the Trullan Synod of 692 until they had been expurgated.[23] For its part, the East sorted out the canons admitted by Rome, accepting some of them and rejecting others, and not always following exactly the same text; the same is true of the canons of the Council of Sardica.

I have already mentioned some cases of non-reception: the non-reception of Chalcedon is all the more significant inasmuch as it did not touch upon essentially profound aspects of christological belief. Later there was the non-reception of the *filioque* clause by the East, the non-reception of the union of Florence by the Orthodox faithful, more or less alarmed by enthusiasts. H. Dombois also cites the example of the extended non-reception of the bull *Execrabilis* of Pius II (1460), which forbade any appeal to the Council (K, pp. 827–8). It also happened that some doctrine or maxim received for a fairly long time might cease so to be accepted: for example, the pope's right to depose monarchs. In our own age, we have the case of the constitution *Veterum sapientia* of John XXIII, prescribing the use of Latin in the instruction of the clergy (1960), and cases of the non-reception of the papal dogma of 18 July 1870 by a number of Catholics, and

---

[22] Cf. A. van Hove, "Droit de Justinien et droit canonique depuis le décret de Gratien (1140) jusju'aux Décrétales de Grégoire IX (1234)": *Miscellanea historica Van der Essen* (Brussels and Paris, 1947), vol. I, pp. 257–71; P. Legendre, *La pénétration du droit romain dans le droit canonique classique de Gratien à Innocent IV (1140–1154)* (Paris, 1964) (thesis); H. D. Hazeltine, *Roman and Canon Law in the Middle Ages* (*Cambridge Medieval History*, vol. V, pp. 697–764).—Gratian, examined by A. Vetulani (*Rev. hist. droit français et étr.*, 1946–47, pp. 11–48), says that "non *recipiuntur*" without discernment everything admitted by the "leges principum": *Dict. post* c. 4, C. XV q. 3 (Friedberg, 752).—Lucius III, c. 1.X 531 (Friedberg II, 844).

[23] Cf. V. Laurent, "L'œuvre canonique du concile in Trullo (691–692), source primaire du droit de l'Eglise orientale", *Rev. Etudes byzant.* 23 (1965), pp. 7–41.

of the teaching of *Humanae Vitae* by a section of the Christian
laity and even of Catholic theologians. Is this "non-reception", or
"disobedience", or what? The facts are there.

II. Some Theories Justifying Reception

In the integral text of the present essay (cf. note 1 above), I examine two theories which have now been abandoned:

(*a*) The theory of the acceptance of laws, held especially by
François Zabarella († 1417), Nicholas of Cusa, and some Gallicans (Pierre Pithou, Pierre de Marca, Claude Fleury).

(*b*) A variation on the preceding theory: the legislator is unwill-
ing to force those subject to him who refuse his ruling. A theory
held by Dominic of St Gemignano († before 1436), Martin of
Aspilcueta († 1586), Escobar y Mendoza († 1669) and, in an extreme formulation ("absque ulla causa!") condemned by Alexander VII, on 26 September 1665 and 18 March 1686 (propos. 28,
DSch 2048.

(*c*) Some considerations of the first Gallicans do seem to be of a
more assuredly ecclesiological interest. The Gallicans liked to
argue from ideas which do not at first seem appropriate or topical,
but which do reveal their depth on the reflective analysis.

"Reception" evidently implied that the local churches, and
local episcopates, were not reduced to the passivity or "blind
obedience" which Bossuet cited. This is why the Gallicans, con-
sidering and then refusing a thesis of papal absolutism, associated reception with a conception of apostolic power expressed in
two biblical texts: authority in Christianity is not domination
(Mt. 20. 26; Lk. 22. 25); power is given "non ad destructionem
sed ad aedificationem" (2 Cor. 13. 10).[24] Those who did not conceive things other than juridically could not understand this as
spirituality or an attitude of piety. A characteristic of Gallican
thought, in addition to a sound historical reference (which, in its

[24] The classic texts of John de Segovia (cf. A. Black, *Monarchy and
Community. Political Ideas Controversy, 1430–1450* [Cambridge, 1970],
pp. 143, 159–60); Pierre de Marca, *De concordia Sacerdotii et Imperii seu
de libertatibus Ecclesiae Gallicanae*, lib. II, c. 16, n. VI, p. 115; Honoré de
Tournély, *De Ecclesia Christi* [Paris, ²1717], q. III, a. 6; Cl. Fleury, *Institution au droit ecclésiastique* [Paris, 1771], vol. II; ch. 2, p. 18 and ch. 25,
pp. 195 ff. (D, p. 202 n. 9).

extreme form, threatened to become a form of archaeologism), was its strong pastoral emphasis. It held to local pastoral structures. It introduced into the theology of power a consideration of its finality and of the use made of it, which was not finalized but conditioned and measured by the good of the Churches. This was commonly admitted in the case of laws: thus, in fact, St Isidore,[25] Gratian[26] and Aquinas.[27] Under such conditions it is impossible to admit at the head of the Church any discretionary and despotic power that would not take into account the good which the Churches and their pastors themselves have at heart, which no one is entitled to counter with a "Cur ita facis?" Since the extraordinary increase of what G. le Bras calls "pontifical domination", the canonists had variously introduced into the law itself the conditions for its reasonable and Christian exercise.[28] This was also the basis of the ecclesiological reactions of Pierre d'Ailly and Gerson, and of the valuable ecclesiology John of Ragusa advanced at the time of the Council of Basle.[29] The texts constantly cited a power (of the pope) given "in aedificationem"—not for the sake of domination, but in order to serve the good of the Church, and for no other end.[30] Such is the sense of the formula according to which the keys were given to the Church (to the "ecclesia") "finaliter".

It ought to be added that in modern theology, the text of 2 Cor. 13. 10, "in aedificationem, non in destructionem" has become a

[25] "Est autem lex honesta, iusta, possibilis, secundum naturam, secundum consuetudinem patriae, loco temporique conveniens, necessaria, utilis ... pro communi utilitate civium conscripta." *Etymol.* lib. V, c. 21 (PL 82, 203).

[26] *Dictum post.* c. 1 D. IV (Friedberg I, 5): "In ipsa constitutione legum maxime qualitas constituendarum est observanda, ut contineant in se honestatem, iustitiam, possibilitatem, convenientiam".

[27] Cf. Ia IIae q. 90, a. 2 and 4; q. 95, a. 3.

[28] Cf. L. Buisson, *Potestas und Caritas. Die päpstliche Gewalt im Spätmittelalter* (Cologne-Graz, 1958).

[29] See his *De Ecclesia*, lib. II, cc. 23 and 32; *Eglise de S. Augustin à l'époque moderne* (*Hist. des dogmes*, III/3) (Paris, 1970), pp. 329–30; by Gerson, pp. 316–20.

[30] Cf. *inter al.*, Pierre d'Ailly, "De Ecclesiae et cardinalium auctoritate", in *Opera Gersonii*, ed. Ellies du Pin" (Antwerp, 1706), vol. II, p. 100; Gerson, *De potestate ecclesiastica, consid.* 1, 8 and 11 (*id. op.* 227, 237 BC, 243 B); *De auferibilitate sponsi (papae) ab Ecclesia* (1409), 12 ff. (215 ff.); *Trialogus de materia schismatis* (83 ff.); *Propos. facta coram Anglicis* (123).

classic source of respect for the order desired by Christ in his Church. It was cited during the sixteenth and seventeenth centuries, by authors who had not a whiff of Gallicanism about them, sometimes even in order to justify the non-obligatory nature of a "non-received" law.[31] The same text was invoked at the First Vatican Council, both by the *de Fide* deputation and by those who wanted the limits of papal power to be laid down.[32]

III. THEOLOGICAL INTERPRETATION AND JUSTIFICATION

"Reception" has suffered from a construction and presentation on the level of constitutional law, like any legal theory. It was also by putting it on the juridical level and by using a dissociative polemical method that Capellari tried to refute the theory, at the risk of ignoring the historical fact and theological depth of reception.[33] This last derives from another level, as noted by P. Fransen, who qualifies it as "organic" in contradistinction not to "juridical" but to purely "jurisdictional" (cf. G, p. 85). It derives from a theology of communion, itself associated with a theology of local churches, a pneumatology and a theology of tradition and a sense of the profound conciliarity of the Church. The notion of reception—but not its whole reality, since life is resistant to theories—is excluded (or even expressly rejected) when for all the foregoing there is substituted a wholly pyramidal conception of the Church as a mass totally determined by its summit, in which (quite apart from any consideration of a largely private spirituality) there is hardly any mention of the Holy Spirit other than as the guarantor of an infallibility of hierarchical courts, and where the conciliar decrees themselves become papal decrees "sacro approbante concilio".[34]

[31] D, p. 224 and n. 60 also cite Gregory of Valence; *Commentaria theologica*, vol. II, disp. VII, q. V punct. V, col. 804 f.; Valerius Reginaldus, *Praxis fori poenitentialis*, lib. XIII, tr. IV, tit. 1, c. 16, n. 160, p. 523. Cf. also, Jemolo, *Chiesa e Stato negli scrittori politici italiani del Seicento e del Settecento* (Turin, 1914), p. 130 ff.

[32] Preparatory Commission (Mansi 49, 707 CD), rep. by: D'Avanzo (Mansi 52, 715 B); Zinelli (52, 1105 CD; 1115 D–1116 A).

[33] *Il trionfo della S. Sede e della Chiesa* (Rome, 1799), chap. XVII.

[34] Cf. Lateran III, Florence, Vatican I, etc. . . .; Lyons I (1245) is presented as a mere amplification of the pope's decision. Cf. G. Alberigo, "Una cum patribus, Ecclesia Spiritu Sancto edocta", *Mélanges théologiques. Hommage à Mgr Gérard Philips* (Gembloux, 1970), pp. 291–319.

RECEPTION AS AN ECCLESIOLOGICAL REALITY   61

This ecclesiological process has been associated with another process that accords with it entirely: the transition from a primacy of truthful content, which it was the grace and mission of the whole Church to protect, to the primacy of an authority. In the theology of tradition it would be put thus: a transition from the *traditio passiva* to the *traditio activa*, or from *traditum* to *tradens*, the latter being identified with what, since the beginning of the eighteenth century, has in fact been called the "teaching Church".[35] I have pointed out that the authority of the "Nicene creed" was attributed not to a "power" of the hierarchical assembly, but to the conformity of its teaching with the faith received from the apostles. Essentially, in the doctrinal area, only the truth has authority. "Hierarchical" ministers exercise no more than a service, a function and a mission (Cajetan, in a commentary on St Thomas, calls the Church "ministra objecti"), it being understood that a mission includes the means necessary for its accomplishment: in this case, grace or charism. But this charism cannot, as such, be interpreted in terms of juridical "power". Such a "power" certainly exists: it is the jurisdictional authority which, in the Church and on behalf of its members, adds to the authentic proposition of truth an obligation which comprises "dogma" and is handed on, in the course of history, by means of an "anthema sit". But the accession of faith, when doctrine is in question, concerns the content of truth. In scholastic terminology, one would say that it concerns the *quod* and not the *quo*. If an *authority* relative to the content of truth as such is attributed to the ministry, one argues upon the juridical level, and the only permissible connection is one of obedience. If the *content* of truth and of good is taken into account, the faithful and, better, the *ecclesia*, may be allowed a certain activity of discernment and "reception".

We may now try to define the theological (ecclesiological) status of "reception" (A), then its legal status, remembering that this legality is still clearly *theological* (B).

[35] See my *La Tradition et les traditions, I. Essai historique* (Paris, 1960) and *"Eglise enseignante", L'Eglise de S. Augustin à l'époque moderne* (Paris, 1970), p. 389. I cite (p. 371), the text of Thomas Stapleton's (†1598): "In doctrina fidei non quid dicatur, sed quis loquetur a fideli populo attendendum est" (*De principiis fidei doctrinalibus*, 1572, lib. X, title of ch. V).

A. The whole body of the Church, which is structured locally as individual churches, is enlivened by the Holy Spirit. The faithful and the churches are true subjects of action and free initiative. Of course there is no true pneumatology without christology: that is, without a normative reference to something given. The Spirit unceasingly renews that which is given, but he does not create anything which is substantially other. One of Sohm's errors is to have conceived a kind of pneumatocracy without given structures. But the faithful and the local churches are not inert and wholly passive in regard to the structures of belief, and ethical and cultic rules that history has necessarily defined since the original apostolic transmission. They have a faculty of discernment, of co-operation with the determination of their forms of life. Of course, in those matters which concern the unity of the Church, and therefore the unity of the faith, all must unite in a substantial unanimity, but they should come to that unity as living independent subjects. Naturally obedience is itself an activity of life and the Holy Spirit inspires it. But not everything is laid down in the tradition of the Church, and the dogmatic formulas themselves require a form of adherence which does not call merely upon volition, but upon intelligence and its conditioning factors, which are culture, knowledge language, and so on. The history of the slow reception of Nicaea or of Chalcedon cannot be explained other than in this context.

Hence we can see that there are two means of arriving at unanimity: obedience, and reception or consent. The first is insisted upon if the Church is conceived as a society subject to a monarchical authority; the second comes into question when the universal Church is seen as a communion of churches. It is certain that this second conception was the one that prevailed effectively during the first thousand years of Christianity, whereas the other one dominated in the West between the eleventh-century reformation and Vatican II.[36] It is true that this rule of local churches in communion with one another was the only form

[36] See my *De la communion des Eglises à une ecclésiologie de l'Eglise universelle: L'Episcopat et l'Eglise universelle* (*Unam Sanctam* 39) (Paris, 1962), pp. 227–60; *L'Ecclésiologie du haut moyen âge. De S. Grégoire le Grand à la désunion entre Byzance et Rome* (Paris, 1968). Other references L, p. 332, n. 30.

possible before the Constantinian peace allowed an open organization of ecumenical life within the framework of the Empire. I admit that another means of unanimity is possible: one by means of submission to a unique head of the Church viewed as a kind of unique and immense diocese.[37] But, apart from the fact that the East and a part of the West never accepted this idea, and never experienced such a form of rule, we have to ask whether it accords with certain aspects of the very nature of the Church, whose authenticity is indefeasible and which Vatican II rediscovered. There are two conditions, supported by numerous witnesses, for this particular ecclesiology:

1. The universal Church cannot err in faith.[38]

2. Consensus, or unanimity, is an effect of the Holy Spirit and the sign of his presence.[39] It is the Holy Spirit who brings about the unity of the Church in space and time; that is, according to the dual dimension of its catholicity and its apostolicity or tradition. It is in fact a matter of acknowledging and expressing the tradition of the Church, in the sense spoken of by Eusebius when (HE V, 28, 6) citing a treatise against the heresy of Artemon. The unanimity which the Councils tried to attain to, and which should not be too idealized, intends this. It does not express a

[37] See the texts cited in *De la communion* (*supra*, n. 36), p. 238 f. Also Gregory IX, letter *Vas ammirabile sol. Gaudemus*, of 13.1.1240 to Queen Georgia de Rusude and her sons David (Potthast 10841), in Baronius-Raynaldus, *Annales eccl.* XXI, pp. 225-6. The Roman Church, as the head of the whole body, is supposed to contain and represent the whole ecclesial body. The same idea appears in St Nicholas I (858–867): "Suscepit ergo et continet in se Romana Ecclesia quod Deus universalem Ecclesiam suscipere ac continere praecipit": *Epist.* 88 (MGH. Epp. VI, p. 480, 15; PL 119, 952), comp. Epist. 90 (p. 498,5).

[38] Texts in O. Rousseau *et al.*, *L'infaillibilité de l'Eglise* (Chevetogne, 1963); G. Thils, *L'infaillibilité du peuple chrétien "in credendo". Notes de théologie posttridentine* (Paris & Louvain, 1963). Cf. St Thomas, II^a II.^{ae} q. 1, a. 9, sed. c.; q. 2 a. 6, ad 3um; Quodl. IX, 16; *Const. Dogm. Lumen gentium* n. 12.

[39] See my article "Konzil als Versammlung und grundsätzliche Konziliarität der Kirche": *Gott in Welt, Festgabe K. Rahner*, vol. II (Freiburg im Br., 1964, pp. 135–65 (p. 152 ff.), reprinted in: *Le Concile au jour le jour. Deuxième session* (Paris, 1964), pp. 9–39. See also, K. Oehler, "Der Consensus omnium als Kriterium der Wahrheit in der antiken Philosophie und der Patristik", *Antike und Abendland* 10 (1961), pp. 103–29, reprinted in K. Oehler, *Antike Philosophie und byzantinisches Mittelalter. Aufsätze zur Gesch. des griech. Denkens* (Munich, 1969), pp. 234–71.

more or less perfect numerical sum of individual ways, but a totality such as that of the memory of the Church. This is the meaning of the formula "ego consensi et subscripsi": I have entered into the consensus which has emerged and by virtue of which it is clear that the Church believes because the truth has been handed down to it in this way. *It is this* which constituted the authority of the Councils in the eyes of the early Fathers of the Church. In this respect, reception is no more than the extension or prolongation of the conciliar process: it is associated with the same essential "conciliarity" of the Church. It may be opined (and this is the basis of the Orthodox position) that the ground of this vision is to be found in "theology", in the sense that the Cappadocian Fathers think of theology: the mystery of the Holy Trinity. If, in trinitarian theology, the consideration of the hypostases is not obscured by an affirmation of the unity of nature, but is instead fully developed, one may also, in ecclesiology, see personal subjects communicating in a unity which is not imposed on them so as to obscure them as individuals. Authority is evidently common to the three Persons, but each of them brings to it his own hypostatic mark, which ought to be reflected in the Church: the monarchy of the Father and the authority of the creator; the submission of the Son exercising his power within a rule of service; the intimacy of the Spirit who inspires initiatives tending to the kingdom of God, and a communion in which each individual is alive to whatever another may reveal to him.

B. It is not reception which bestows their legitimacy upon a conciliar decision and an authentic decree: they obtain their legitimation and their obligatory value from the authorities who have supported them. As H. Dombois remarks: "Reception always has to do with a previous fact offered to the one who receives it as possessing an obligatory value" (K, p. 827). Even though reception creates neither legitimacy nor a legal force of obligation, one has had immediately to add that, in the soundest Christian tradition, those *ministers exercising authority never act alone.*[40] This was true of the apostles: cf. Acts 15. 2–23 and 16. 4;

[40] See J. A. Möhler, *L'unité dans l'Eglise ou le principe du Catholicisme d'après l'esprit des Pères des trois premiers siècles,* § 16. Trad. A. de Lilienfeld (*Unam Sanctam* 2) (Paris, 1938), pp. 28 ff.; Darwell Stone, *The Christian Church* (London, ³1915), pp. 333 ff.; Y. Congar, *Jalons pour une théologie du laïcat* (*Unam Sanctam,* 23) (Paris, 1953), esp. chap. V.

2 Tim. 1. 6 and 1. Tim. 4. 14; 1 Cor. 5. 4–5, where it is possible to discern an application of the communitarian discipline reported in Mt. 18. 17–20 (see also Clement, Cor. 44. 3). This was true of the bishops of the age of the martyrs, Ignatius of Antioch[41] and Cyprian.[42] The basis for this, well brought out by Möhler, is that a Christian always has need of a Christian brother: he has to be supported or confirmed by another, and, as much as possible, by a community. This is the basis of the "fraternal correction" which is also a real aspect of the life of the Church. The principle enunciated in Dt. 19. 15 on the necessity of two or three witnesses was taken up in the New Testament in a way that goes beyond the juridical or procedural framework, and assumes a general value as a rule of Christian behaviour.

If reception confers neither legitimacy nor an obligatory value, what does it do? R. Sohm says that it is an open process, and juridically very unsatisfactory:[43] this is very true. In addition, he attributes to it a purely declaratory value, "the significance of attestation". It attests that these decisions really arise from the Spirit which directs the Church, and that they are of value for the Church as such (and not primarily by virtue of their reception).[44] I am not far from subscribing to this formula: Bossuet also says, speaking of the judgments made by the bishop of Rome: "Since he is in effect at the head of the ecclesial communion, and since his definition intends nothing other than what he knows to be the feeling of all the churches, the subsequent consent only attests that everything has been done in due order and in accordance with truth."[45] H. Dombois, however, notes rightly that, in Sohm, this interpretation is connected with the same author's general thesis: in the early Church there was no *law*, but merely recognition of the action of the Spirit: "Sohm interpreted the concept of reception in an extrajuridical (*ausserrechtlich*) manner" (K, p. 826). Therefore Sohm would not escape criticism, but less for what he says than for what he omits to say. Perhaps Paul

---

[41] Cf. Ephes. 20; Magnes. 6, 7; Trall. 3.

[42] Cf. Epist. 14, 4; 55, 8, 5. Cf. *Jalons*, pp. 329 ff. and 335.

[43] *Das altkatholische Kirchenrecht und das Dekret Gratians (Festschrift der Leipziger juristen-Fakultät für A. Wach.* (Munich & Leipzig, 1918) (reprinted: Darmstadt, 1967), p. 134.

[44] *Kirchenrecht* I (Leipzig, 1892), p. 320.

[45] *Dissertatio praevia* of 1696 to the Gallican clergy, n. 78.

Hinschius offers a better appreciation of the situation. In regard to the ecumenical councils of the first millennium, he remarks: "Reception is not an action which brings about validity and constitutes it in principle; it merely declares that decisions have been valid since the beginning; non-reception, on the other hand, does not harm the perfection of validity (juridical validity, that is); instead, it affirms that decisions have been null since their making."[46]

Reception is not constitutive of the juridical quality of a decision. It has no bearing on the formal aspect of the action, but on its content. It does not confer validity, but affirms, acknowledges and attests that this matter is for the good of the Church: because it concerns a decision (dogma, canons, ethical rules) that should ensure the good of the Church. This is why the reception of a Council is practically identical with its efficacy, as may be seen from Lateran IV, Trent, and even Nicaea, Chalcedon or Nicaea II. On the other hand, as Ph. Bacht remarks, non-reception does not mean that the decision given is a false one. It means that this decision does not call forth any living power and therefore does not contribute to edification:[47] for religious truth, and what is sometimes called the development of dogma, do not derive from a pure conceptuality of the mathematical or geometrical type; they derive from what tradition calls "pietas fidei" or "veritas secundum pietatem" (in reference to 1 Tim. 6. 3; 3. 16; Tit. 1. 1; Rom. 1. 18) or, in St Thomas, "sacra doctrina", "doctrina salutaris".

Distinctions have sometimes been made between power and authority. Power is juridical, it is a right; it has been defined as "the possibility that a man has of making his idea and his will prevail over those of others in a determined social system". Authority is spiritual or moral; it is an efficacious process of extension and transmission. There may be such a thing as a power without authority, but an authority without "power" may also be held and exercised: what, for example, is to be thought of St Cyprian,

[46] *Das Kirchenrecht der Katholiken und Protestanten in Deutschland*, vol. III/1 (Berlin, 1879), p. 349.

[47] H. Bacht, "Vom Lehramt der Kirche und in der Kirche", *Catholica* 25 (1971), pp. 144–67 (pp. 157 ff.: "Das Problem der Rezeption im katholischen Verständnis").

of whom Gregory of Nazianzen said: "He does not exercise his presidency over the Church of Carthage and Africa and no other, but over the whole region of the West and over almost all those of the East, from the South to the North, wherever his marvellous fame has reached."[48] One might also cite Isidore or Thomas Aquinas, but above all Augustine, bishop of a city of average size, who for more than a thousand years determined the countenance of Christianity in the West.

The ideal would be an overlapping of the two: a certain authority, in the above-mentioned sense, should always be accorded to the act of power. Thanks to God, that has often happened. I would cite in this regard St Gregory, or St Leo, to whom we owe this formula: "Etsi diversa nonnunquam sunt merita praesulum (spiritual authority!), iura tamen permanent sedium (power!)."[49]

Once again we meet with juridicism: reception no longer has any place in a conception where formal juridical authority takes up all the space, without any consideration of the content of its decisions. On the other hand, in this perspective of recognition by the Church of what is good for it, we ought to listen to those conciliarist churchmen or Gallicans already cited when they speak of the idea of a power not of domination but of service, given "ad aedificationem", finalized and measured by the good of the Church.

But certain qualified defenders of papal monarchy also introduce some interesting considerations. Thomas de Vio (Cajetan) asks what the Council may add to the pope, when he answers the Gallican Jacques Almain. The answer is: nothing, from the viewpoint of the degree of authority, but something, and indeed a large thing, in regard to the richness and extension of the doctrine, for its acceptance without opposition and thus by all.[50] Cajetan's predecessor, like him a Dominican, Juan de Torquemada, acknowledged that in a case of extreme doubt respecting

[48] *Oratio* XXIV, 12 in Laud. Cypr. (PG 35, 1184).
[49] *Epist. 106 ad Anatolium* (Jaffé-Kaltenbrunner 483; PL 54, 1007 B); 119 ad Maxim. Antioch., 3 (Jaffé-K. 495; col. 1043 A).
[50] *Apologia de comparata auctoritate Papae et Concilii*, c. XI (1514): ed. V. M. I. Pollet (Rome, 1936), n. 636, p. 269.

a matter of faith, a Council had to be summoned. In answer to
the objection that this would imply that a Council was of more
account than a pope, Torquemada remarked that this was not so
in the case of a greater power of jurisdiction and when the pope
was incontestable (even though he was writing in 1457, he had
experienced the situation that arose from the great Western
schism); on the other hand, it was true of a greater authority of
faculty of judgment: for a Council was held to be able to bring
to its deliberations more reasoning power than a single man.[51]
Torquemada composed a reply to the demand of Charles VII of
France, who wanted a third general Council to be held beginning
in 1442). The bishop of Meaux, Pierre de Versailles, ambassador
of Charles VII to the pope on this point (16 December 1441), put
forward the following argument: there are two kinds of authority, that of the *power* that one has received, and that of the
credence (or credibility) that one may enjoy. Although power is
the same power in the case of all pontiffs, the credence accorded
each of them differs: St Gregory and St Leo had more than others,
and the general Council is superior in this respect.[52] This is very
like the distinction I have suggested between "power" and "authority". The concept of "credence" or "credibility" is in favour
today. It may certainly be used to characterize the support that
reception gives to a decision that is legitimate in itself.

Hinschius spoke of a "confirmation" (*Bewährung*) by means
of reception. We may accept this term, not in the technical, i.e.,
legal sense (as when, for example, one speaks of the confirmation
of an election by a higher authority or court: CIC, can. 177), but
in the sense of the increased effectiveness that the consent of the
affected parties gives to a decision.[53]

Translated by John Griffiths

---

[51] Ioannes a Turrecremata, *In Gratiani Decretorum primam Commen-
tarii*: in D.XIX, c. 8 (Venetiis, 1578), p. 176a).

[52] Dans Baronius-Raynaldus, Annales; ed. Theiner, t. XXVIII, p. 363
(n. 10).

[53] Compare this comment of St Albert the Great on Apoc. 5, 14: "Duplex
est confirmatio: per ratificationem, et haec est auctoritas et pertinet ad
majores. Alia est par approbationem et consensum, et haec pertinet ad
minores" (*Opera*, ed. Borgnet, vol. XXXVIII, p. 571).

Wilhelm Kölmel

Episcopal Elections and
Political Manipulation

WHEN, in contemporary discussions of renewal, a demand is made
for elected bishops, we must look at the history of the Church if
we are to avoid an uncritical use of utopian political models.
Therefore I shall examine here both the Church's attitude to
elections, and its experiences with the State in the centuries leading up to our own.

In 1454, for example, Scholarios was elected patriarch of Constantinople, possibly at the instigation of Mohammed II. The
sultan handed over the crozier; it was a gloomy scene, and one
which introduced a period of weakness in the face of the Turks.
Patriarchs continued to be elected, in theory by free elections,
though in fact they had to have the sultan's approval, with the
result that only acceptable candidates were considered. The situation, highlighted by the sultan's being of another faith, seems
less peculiar if we think of the pseudo-elections under the foreign
Frankish Merovingians, or the times when the king appointed
bishops or confirmed their elections. A vivid letter from John X
(921) reported by Santifaller shows how this was accepted as
normal.[1] The pope rebukes Hermann of Cologne for having un-
canonically consecrated a certain Hilduin as bishop of Liège out
of fear of Count Gislebert: "... without election by the clergy or
the consent of the people ... whereas ancient custom requires
that no one shall confer a diocese on a cleric except the king, who

[1] L. Santifaller, *Zur Geschichte des ottonischen-salischen Reichskirchen-
systems* (Vienna, 1964), pp. 118 ff.

has received the sceptre from God." John emphasizes his deep distress at Gislebert's behaviour in a letter to the West Carolingian Charles III, combining it with a profession of reverence for the monarchy: "... since ancient custom and the noble rank of the monarchy decreed (*censuit*) that no one should consecrate a bishop without the king's authority."[2]

This statement dates from a period of weakness on the part of the hierarchy and the papacy. The pressure on the papacy in connection with appointments to the papal and episcopal offices increased in the Ottonian period, but in the eleventh century we begin to hear of "lay investiture". The complaints of the reformers extend from the *Ordinatio Imperii*, via Humbert and Peter Damian to the investiture controversy itself. The reformers' attack on the existing practice of episcopal investiture was also an attack on the system of royal power in the Church (*rex in ecclesia*) which had grown up since the Constantinian settlement. It was an attack which would inevitably lead to a radical change in the ecclesiastical and political order, including episcopal appointments, as is shown by Paschal II's offer to surrender the temporalities. But Paschal failed, and in the Concordat of Worms the imperial party won the right of *praesentia* at elections (the Calixtine concession) on imperial territory. This compromise was a sign of the tendency that was later to produce the disputes and compromises between the two powers, the *sacerdotium* and the *regnum*. It also destroyed the possibility, which had emerged in the early stages of the Gregorian reform, of a renewal of the system of episcopal appointments based on an idealized model of the early Church.

This is not the place for a detailed discussion of the historical status of this ideal, which became embodied in the formula "canonical election". It is simply a fact that the reform derived its impetus from attitudes which looked back from the domination of the Church by emperor and kings to a time when the Church made its appointments "freely"; this is the context in which the idea of *electio* appears. In connection with the election of bishops, however, the phrase "election by *clerus et populus*",

---

[2] W. Kölmel, *Regimen Christianum, Weg und Ergebnisses des Gewalten-verständnisses und Gewaltenverhältnisses* (Berlin, 1970), pp. 69 ff.

still more than a cliché at this period, comes to mind automatically. How far the concept of "canonical election" fits, or was meant to be identical with, the historical situation implied by the phrase "election by clergy and people" is a question I shall simply note and leave on one side.

What is certain is that the early reform was introduced under the slogan *electio cleri et populi* (Synod of Rheims, 1049) and that Gregory VII, who was himself dragged to the papal throne after "a great uproar among the people", still thought and acted in these terms (Reg. IV, 14, 22). It is impossible to give an interpretation of the concept of canonical election and of its relation to "election by clergy and people" adequate to the importance of the problem. On the contrary, a look at the history of the formula *clerus et populus*, which still dominated the thinking of Gregory VII, shows how this principle became an empty formula. In Gratian's *Decretum* there is a clear tendency to eliminate the "people" from the election.[3]

This conceptual awareness foreshadows the further development, in a totally different direction from the early reforming attempts to make the *ecclesia* active as a community by setting clergy and people in opposition to the power of the nobles. *Electio* is visibly either restricted to colleges, reduced to the right to propose names, or simply ignored. We see how Gratian's conception came to seem natural. Three lines can be distinguished.

(*a*) The election of the bishop becomes a matter for the chapter; the emergence of the right to elect the pope as restricted to the college of cardinals may have provided an analogy. In the chapters, canonical election becomes chapter election, and thereby open to secular influences as a result of the generally élitist composition of chapters. Chapters formed a high-ranking, noble or noble-bourgeois group, and as such were directly tied to the class which was the junior partner in the feudal power structure. The history of noble chapters in German-speaking territories up to 1803 is a good illustration of this.

(*b*) On the other hand, Rome tried to bring episcopal appointments under its own control, and this tendency was supported by the theory which grew up in canon law of the constitutive

[3] R. L. Benson, *The Bishop Elect* (Princeton, 1968), pp. 33 ff.

necessity of *confirmatio* by a *superior*. As the centralized papal system developed, this process prevailed in many forms, except where the secular powers reacted by trying to enforce their old influence on episcopal elections. From this point of view, episcopal appointments developed over the centuries into a conflict between Rome and the princes.

(*c*) The ways in which the secular side sought, and gained, victory in this struggle were determined by developments within the Church. The right of presence at an election granted to the king by the Concordat of Worms gave him a measure of influence over the chapter. Adalbert of Mainz, one of the negotiators of 1122, was soon complaining that as a result of this presence "God's Church has to suffer the same slavery as before, or perhaps in even more oppressive form". After the Würzburg Reichstag in 1133, Konrad of Salzburg complained in a letter to Norbert of Magdeburg about the role of leading laymen (*honorati*) in episcopal elections. Among those mentioned are the "governors" (*Vögte*), which probably means "local rulers". Chapters were not in a position to carry out their *canonica electio* freely. In France, the king made extensive use of the *licentia eligendi,* or recognition of an election. Before his departure for the Third Crusade (1190), Philip II Augustus issued the following *Ordonnance*: "When a see or a royal abbey becomes vacant, it is our wish that the canons of the church or the monks of the vacant monastery should come to the king and the archbishop and ask them for a free election. And we command that they be granted this without reservation. But we remind the canons and the monks that they are to choose a priest who is pleasing to God and useful to the realm (*utilis sit regno*). The king and the archbishop may keep the temporalities until the person elected is consecrated or blessed, when they shall be given to him without hesitation." An episcopal election under the slogan *utilis regno* implies not only the political and social responsibility of the hierarchical office-holder, but his dependence on a monarchical and feudal environment.

The various possibilities of influencing episcopal elections outlined above enter a new situation as Church and State take up new positions under the pressure of serious crises. For the papal absolutism now developing in theory and in practice, and for the connected fiscal and administrative centralization, such a crisis was presented by the Schism, the reforming councils dominated by conciliarist theory and finally by the Reformation itself. The secular side was similarly affected by wars and the later secular "reformation", the revolutions, with their structural crises. Ecclesiastical and secular crises and reforms affected episcopal appointments by their general aims. The reforming Councils of Constance and Basle which ended the schism with their attack on curial centralism—Basle rejected all general reservations not contained in the code of canon law—offered an opportunity to restore the election of bishops to its position in the early Church. But such a radical reform was not attempted, and events moved in a different direction, influenced largely by the growing power of local and national rulers. It was the declared aim of the secular side to bring episcopal appointments under their control through nomination. The right of the chapters to elect came under even greater pressure and was left finally with a very limited scope. The papacy, threatened by the confusion in the Church, tried to preserve the hierarchical unity of the Church by means of privileges, with the result that the modern State became the greatest beneficiary of the Church's crisis.

As regards the chapters' right of election, the Concordat of Vienna (1448) granted *electiones canonice*, and guaranteed this right in the territory of the former kingdom of the *natio Alemanica*. At the same time, however, individual rulers (the groups of dioceses of Brandenburg and Meissen) obtained the right to nominate bishops, and the emperor acquired this privilege for some newly established dioceses (Vienna, Vienna Neustadt and, alternately with Salzburg, Gurk). Where the right of nomination was not secured, there was still a possibility of influencing the election directly, and from this tendency came the practice of excluding "less acceptable persons" (*persona minus grata*) from elections. In Spain, as Alvaro Pelayo had complained in the fourteenth century, kings were able to influence elections by presenting their candidates to the electors, a procedure which became the rule in Castile. An opportunity for this form of presentation was offered by the *exhortatio* to the electors which preceded the voting, which could easily become a speech in favour

of the royal candidate.[4] Another practice which became an instrument of the royal will was the petitioning of candidates
directly to Rome, as in Aragon, where it could also be derived from
the right of patronage over the dioceses won in the *conquista*.
This patronage, made universal by Innocent VIII in 1486 ("full
right of patronage and the right to present suitable persons"),
represents the most extreme extension of the right of nomination.

In Europe, France obtained the right of nomination to ninety-
three dioceses in return for the repeal of the Pragmatic Sanction
of Bourges. Cathedral chapters opposed this surrender of their
rights, and their opposition did not die out until the sixteenth
century. The dominant influence of the monarchy also included
the rights of noble families, as can be seen from the rise of Richelieu. Henri III had put the diocese of Luçon in the gift of the
family, and Richelieu's elder brother Armand was appointed
bishop by the king, but renounced the appointment on the day
of the investiture. Richelieu himself was now solemnly elected,
and the king applied to Rome for a dispensation from his
minority. This system of nomination worked as long as there
were no crises, but under Louis XIV a conflict arose over the
temporal possessions of the Church. The diocese of Pamiers,
whose bishop, Gaulet, had been an opponent of the king, was
left empty after Gaulet's death. Louis refused to acknowledge
the vicar general elected by the chapter and appointed a sup-
porter, the Abbé Bourelmont. Innocent XII replied by demand-
ing that the canons who had been punished by Louis should be
restored.

Later, in the dispute over the Four Articles (1682), after the
pope had refused to confirm the appointments of royal supporters,
Louis forbade bishops appointed by him from seeking confirmation of their appointments from Rome in the future. In three
dioceses (Metz, Toul and Verdun), by invoking the Concordat
of 1516, he eliminated the rights of the chapters for all practical
purposes. Louis's actions are certainly an extreme case of the
Catholic form of absolutism, but none the less show the possibilities of nomination. In this situation papal confirmation could
protect the freedom of the Church.

[4] T. de Azcona, *La elección y Reforma del episcopado español en tempo
de los Reyes católicos* (Madrid, 1966), pp. 64–5; 306–7.

The secular side also made attempts to encroach where the rights of chapters were guaranteed by a Concordat, as in the territory covered by the Concordat of Vienna. From the eighteenth century onwards it became customary in the churches of the empire for an imperial commissioner to make known the emperor's wishes at the election, though he was not permitted to be present during voting. In addition, the Wittelsbachs and Hapsburgs made use of the office of coadjutor to win control of a number of dioceses, and noble families such as the Schönborns gained control of appointments in another group of dioceses (Mainz, Würzburg, Bamberg). Such concentrations of power were made possible by the noble composition of the chapters.

Episcopal appointments and elections entered the nineteenth and twentieth centuries in historical conditions derived from the *ancien régime*. Papal appointment or confirmation, royal nomination, especially in Catholic countries, with chapter election in between with constantly diminishing scope constituted the range. The election of constitutional bishops in revolutionary France remained an isolated episode. The question with which the emancipation and constitutional crises brought about by the Great Revolution faced Church, State and society was this: What form will episcopal appointments take in a changing world, and what will become of the old model of canonical election? Two answers were given.

(*a*) On the papal side, the process visible since the investiture controversy ended in canon 329, 2 of the 1917 code of canon law: "They (bishops) are freely appointed by the bishop of Rome", though in 329,3 election by chapters and, in 331,2 and 332,4, nomination were mentioned as possible concessions.

(*b*) Governments still attempted to retain old rights of nomination, even if in different forms, and also tried to maintain their influence in chapter elections; the imperial practice of the eighteenth century is a good example.

An extension of the right of nomination can be seen in Austria, at first in individual acts (Bressanone, Trent, Venetia, Ragusa), then in 1855 in all the imperial states (except Olmütz and Salzburg), and in Bavaria (the Concordat of 1817). In France the Concordat of 1801 had restored nomination (article 5) in a more clearly defined but disastrously intensified form with the requirement that all bishops in office should be asked to resign (article 3). The Concordat survived the political changes until the separation of Church and State in 1905, and under the Third Republic gave rise to an interesting variant whereby before the nomination a consultation about the nominee took place between the nuncio and the government (the *entente préalable*). Similar attempts by the nuncio in Austria remained unsuccessful, but in this case the emperor was obliged (by article 19 of the 1855 Concordat) to consult the local bishops.

The right of election by chapter was still provided for by law in some areas (Prussia, Hanover, the church province of the Upper Rhine and Switzerland), but the practice of the governments of the German states shows very clearly the true situation of the chapters in the face of authorities committed to a policy of subordinating the Church to the State. Secularization and the new order in the Church had ended the influence of the nobles over the chapters in the churches of the empire, and this had freed the chapters from their involvement with the ruling classes.

The bull of circumscription, *De salute animarum* (1821), now confirmed the rights of the chapters, though the brief *Quod de fidelium* added the rider that only such persons should be elected as were known not to be *minus grati*. With the change to the "Irish system", under which a list of candidates was submitted to the government so that undesirable names could be eliminated, the State's influence in Hanover, and the Upper Rhine church province was firmly established (1824, 1827). Wilhelm III made his right of exclusion in practice a right of participation by regularly announcing to the chapters the name of the candidate he favoured, who was then elected. It was only under his successor, Wilhelm IV (from 1840 onwards), that the use of the list was introduced. In Hessen until 1899 an electoral commissioner regularly took part in the elections, and this produced a notable intervention on the election of Moufang as vicar capitular after Kettler's death (1877). Moufang was not recognized, and the see of Mainz remained empty until 1886.[5] A similar situation arose

[5] L. Lenhart, "Moufangs Ablehnung als Kapitelsvikar", *Archiv für Mittelrheinische Kirchengeschichte* 19 (1967), pp. 157–91; H. E. Feine, *Kirchliche Rechtsgeschichte. Die Katholische Kirche* (Cologne & Graz, ⁴1964), pp. 613 ff.

out of the *Kulturkampf* in Baden, where after the death of von Vicari (1868) so many candidates were declared *minus grati* in the two lists submitted by the chapter in 1868 and 1874 that the required number for a canonical election could not be found. The result was a vacancy of fourteen years. This is the context of Rampolla's letter of 1900, which directed that chapter not to permit either direct or indirect infringements of the freedom of the election.[6]

The political transformation which followed the First World War not only removed the right of nomination (Austria, Bavaria), but revealed, with the newly codified papal right of appointment, a desire to remove the rights of chapters. A first attempt by the Curia in Cologne failed, and in spite of later efforts the new state concordats (with Bavaria, Prussia and Baden) left the rights of chapters in existence, though limiting them by means of the obligation to submit a list of candidates. Hitler was able to take over this rule and link it with the important right to express reservations before the promulgation of the bull of appointment. Formally, this was not supposed to be a veto (article 14), but inevitably acted as a bar. In the case of the Protestant Reichsbischof Müller, Hitler even had the election carried out on a party basis.

The material we have considered allows a clear answer to our question. It is obvious that elections have not prevented political forces from exercising an influence. They do not provide a guarantee for decisions taken purely out of concern for the Church, nor can they provide such a guarantee if the political and social environment has its own interest in hierarchical appointments. Even in a situation where there is no directly political interest, elections can only take place in freedom from pressure if no pressure groups are active. There is, of course, the further question, whether the unrestricted right of papal appointment is a better protection against political manipulation. The arrangements under the 1929 Italian Concordat, which requires an inquiry whether any general political objections exist (article 19, 2), still leave wide scope for political influence, even if it is not publicly apparent. The Spanish Convention of 1941, which

[6] *Archiv für Katholisches Kirchenrecht* 81, pp. 525 ff.

allowed the head of state to choose from a papal list of three, once more highlights the problems of nomination rights. By granting these rights, against the wishes of the reformers, and by the suppression of elections, Rome created a Church-State compact which resulted in an episcopate acceptable to the State dominating the political landscape. How far political preferences penetrate the tortuous channels of papal appointments when there is no overt political influence through nominations, remains a matter for speculation, and this cannot give historians a sufficient basis for interpretation. The fact none the less remains that as a result of the suppression of elections which has been apparent since the investiture controversy, papal appointment has had to bear the whole political and historical burden of resisting the variety of secular attempts to gain influence. Whether the curial system is adequate to this task, and more suited to it than elections, a later age will be in a better position to judge; for the present we may doubt. The new archbishop of Madrid, Tarancón, insisted at his enthronement that his nomination was not the product of politics, even of Church politics, but a sign of the Church's desire to renew itself in order to be closer to the realities of the world,[7] but we have seen that for a long time in the Church such renewal included the active participation of the people at elections, either in the choice itself or in their expression of agreement. This is the meaning of the words of Celestine I: *"Nullus invitis detur episcopus."*

Translated by Francis McDonagh

---

[7] *La documentation Catholique* 54 (1972), p. 168.

Walter Ullmann

The Election of the Bishops and the Kings of France in the Ninth and Tenth Centuries

THE victory of the ecclesiological theme and thought in Frankish realms as a result of the Carolingian Renaissance (considered primarily as a social-collective and only secondarily as an intellectual regeneration or rebirth)[1] has, for reasons irrelevant to this essay, left its indelible imprint in the West-Frankish portion of the former Carolingian empire: that is, in the parts which in due course were to become Capetian France, In this context what is of quite especial interest is the interaction between ecclesiologically based axioms and the tradition, practices and usages that had grown up before the impact of ecclesiologically based principles had made itself felt. For one of the most ancient ecclesiological postulates epitomizing, so to speak, the whole ecclesial theme, concerned the creation of the ecclesiastical officers, notably of the bishops by clergy and people, that is, by the two parts which constituted the Church itself. The manifestation of the idea of representation may well be seen in this postulate. This idea was no stranger within the ascending theme of government as practised in the Germanic period,[2] and it was to become operational again in the modern period. The ecclesiological postulate was raised to the level of a principle which was said to have its roots in the Old Testament and was at any rate applied in practice during the early Christian centuries.

[1] W. Ullmann, *The Carolingian Renaissance and the Idea of Kingship* (London, 1969), pp. 5–69.
[2] *Id.*, *Principles of Government and Politics in the Middle Ages* (London, ²1966), pp. 20–26.

79

Although throughout the early Frankish period the participation of clergy and people in the election of the bishops was never
disputed, let alone denied, the principle was in practice disregarded. There was an almost unrestricted right on the part of
the king to appoint the bishops: of any articulated opposition to
the royal measures there is no evidence. But from the mid-ninth
century onwards there was noticeable a marked difference between the West-Frankish portion of the Carolingian inheritance
and its East-Frankish parts, the later Germany. Although a
number of reasons can be given for this divergent development,
one of the most persuasive and effective seems to have been the
intellectual advance and maturity that was observable in France
during the ninth and tenth centuries before the advent of Hugh
Capet. The intellectual state of affairs was incomparably higher in
the West than in the Eastern—German—parts. It was this highly
developed, if not sophisticated French intellectualism—Agobard
of Lyons, Jonas of Orléans, Hincmar of Rheims spring to mind
—which was able to restore in some degree the ancient but by
then largely disused electoral principle by virtue of which both
clergy and people became active. The difficulties which the
higher ecclesiastics either on their own or when assembled in
the numerous synods experienced in their attempt to win recognition of this principle should not be underestimated. For the so-
called proprietary church system which by virtue of the agrarian
bases and land-owning foundations of contemporary society was
firmly entrenched, had also in this context made inroads into
the manipulation of the ecclesiastical mechanics.

This system greatly facilitated the direct royal appointments
of bishops, as indeed it also facilitated the episcopal (or any
clerical) appointment by the lower placed lay lords. And lastly
there was an almost perpetual state of public insecurity, disorder
if not also local chaos, all features which tended to support the
practice of episcopal appointments by the king, if only for reasons
of expediency. An example is the famous letter which (obviously
on behalf of the king, Charles the Bald) Archbishop Wenilo of
Sens and Count Gérard of Vienne addressed to the archbishop
of Lyons requesting him to consecrate the two men chosen by
the king for the vacant sees of Autun and Chalons. One of the
significant reasons advanced was that large-scale public disturb-

ances had prompted the king to act,[3] and it was a royal duty to bring to an end this perilous state of affairs by appointing ecclesiastical leaders of the dioceses vacant. It is true that this letter also contains some more general rationalizations for the royal step, but they were clearly put forward only with a view to making palatable the actual royal motivation. This instance may serve as a demonstration for not only the king's exercise of his powers in the public-ecclesiastical field, for which no basis in law or in doctrine could be found, but for the uneasiness which the royal quarter itself sensed in the matter.

Yet there can be no doubt, leaving aside exceptional circumstances or abnormal situations, that the principle of episcopal election by clergy and people was attempted to be made operational throughout the ninth century. The vacancies at Rheims in 845, at Rennes in 866, Chalons in 868, Tours in 869, Laon in 876, were filled, according to narrative and official sources, by election in the canonical manner.[4] Where, however, a change occurred was not in the principle itself, but in the mechanics by which this principle came to be applied. There was the attempt to reconcile legitimately held royal functions—manifesting themselves in the swift provision of the chief ecclesiastical officer for the diocese in order to end a state of public uncertainty—with the no less legitimate participation of the Christian populace—manifesting itself in clergy and people being activated as true electors and thus representing the will of those who were to be governed by the future diocesan.

A compromise had to be found which accorded a sphere of functions to the king as the supreme ruler and public governing organ, distinguished by divinity as the possessor of divine grace and thus as the Lord's anointed, and which also accorded another sphere of functions to the clergy and people as the subjects of the king and the future bishop. The compromise involved the adjustment of the descending theme of government to its ascending counterpart. Thereby the idea of representation and consent (inherent in the ascending theme) as well as the idea of appointment

---

[3] *Monumenta Germaniae Historica: Epistolae*, VI, no. 81, p. 73, lines 16–17: "... *prolixa perturbatio flexit eius (scil. regis) pietatem.*"

[4] G. Weise, *Königtum und Bischofswahl im fränkischen und deutschen Reich vor dem Investiturstrait* (Berlin, 1912), p. 45, note 3.

"from above" (the main feature of the descending theme) could be given an appropriate standing. This doctrinal attempt at a compromise must, evidently, be seen against the contemporary background of insecurity, confusion, disorder, which made the bishops assembled at Meaux in 845 adopt a purely temporizing measure by which they conceded to the king (in view of the prevailing perilous conditions) the right to bring to an end an episcopal vacancy speedily, the reason being that where there is no governor, the people will suffer ruin and the well-being of the soul is more important than that of the body.[5]

But, even as a purely temporizing measure, this synodal decision was short-lived, since it all too blatantly disregarded the ancient canonical requirement of involving clergy and laity actively in the creation of the bishop by means of a free and canonical election. The undoubted leader of the episcopal front was Hincmar of Rheims, who never wavered in his views that the proper organs for creating a bishop was the clergy and people of the diocese. He was too good a jurist not to have known the canon of the Church, and he was well enough versed in history and patristic literature to realize that this was not only the law, but also the practice in early Christian times. Due to the influence of Hincmar and his advocacy of the ancient electoral principle the matter was taken up by the synod of Valence in 855 which found a middle way between the ancient canonical rules and Germanic customs: the synod found a viable compromise. The compromise preserved the right of election by clergy and people, but this was contingent upon the permission of the king, that is to say, clergy and people could not act as electors until and unless the king had given the signal to proceed. This came to be known as the *congé d'élire*.

The reason which this synod advanced was that since recent practice had shown how unworthy and unlettered or uneducated persons had become bishops, a new method was called for, and

[5] *Monumenta Germaniae Historica: Capitularia*, II, 399, repeating the identical view expressed at the synod of Diedenhofen in 844: "*Ubi non est gubernator, populus corruit* (cf. Prov. XI, 14), *et tanto periculosius quanto anima plus est preciosa quam corpus.*" That this measure was considered temporizing is proved by the rubric: "*quaedam movenda subiungimus; quaedam autem pro tempore tunc dicenda nunc brevitate studentes recidimus.*"

the method suggested was to approach the king with the request "that he should now permit the canonical election by clergy and people".[6] When this was obtained, consultations should begin amongst the clergy as well as the people so that a suitable person could be chosen "with the consent of the whole clergy and people".[7] The essential feature here clearly is the consent of both clergy and people.

The *material ingredient* of the creation of the bishop was the *consent* given by the local clergy and people, while the royal *congé d'élire* was viewed as an antecedent, *formal, procedural requirement* which accorded to the king some standing within the ecclesial structure. And the ecclesiological theme had found some concrete and practical manifestation: the function of the king as God's chosen ruler and as the *Christus Domini* to whom divinity had entrusted the kingdom, as well as the role of clergy and people demanded as this role was by canonical requirements and ancient practice, could thus be reconciled and accommodated within the ecclesiological framework. To each relevant part of the Church—secular ruler; clergy; laity—was allocated a legitimate function within the structure of the Church. The motive for this arrangement was to obtain the consent in one of the most vital contingencies of the actual life of the Church, that is, in the creation of the bishop as the leader of his diocese. It was a very remarkable achievement, combining as it did the theocratic ingredient of rulership (showing itself in the *congé d'élire* which was held to be a formal concession) with the material ingredient of the election, the will of the Christian people (the *voluntas populi christiani* manifesting itself in the participation of both clergy and people), who thus acted as representative organs of the whole diocese.

In a word, election and consent had become the emanation of a properly understood ecclesiological point of view. The same synod of Valence in the same decree went as far as to say that even if a cleric who was in the royal service was dispatched to

---

[6] J. D. Mansi, *Sacrorum conciliorum amplissima collectio*, XV, col. 7, ch. 7, which sets forth the principle of suitability continuing: "*a principe supplicando postuletur ut canonicam electionem clero et populo ipsius civitatis permittere dignetur.*"

[7] *Ibid.*

fill a vacant bishopric, the metropolitan should nevertheless institute inquiries about his suitability, and upon suggestion by clergy and people the ruler should permit a free and canonical election of a suitable candidate. If, however, the ruler insisted upon his choice, a subsequent election (which was juristically envisaged as a *ratihabitio*) could still preserve, even only formally, the canonical standpoint. This indeed seems to have been the case with Aeneas of Paris who in 857 was, ostensibly, elected by clergy and people, after having been in no uncertain terms suggested by the king as bishop of Paris.[8]

Special attention should be directed to the continued and determined attempts by Hincmar to curtail the significance of the royal concession in the shape of the *congé d'élire*. He advocated the disregard of this concession which to him was nothing but a formality. And indeed this point of view in somewhat modified form was afterwards adopted when the kings—French as well as German, and also later others—granted numerous electoral privileges which in themselves were on the juristic level nothing else but grants of immunities to churches and monasteries. It was in these electoral privileges granted by the king that the theocratic concession principle had found its constitutional habitat. This development was thus of considerable importance within the ecclesiological sphere and very neatly joined together the elements of election and consensus. The arrangement bore all the marks of practical wisdom and statesmanship.

What, however, on the purely historical plane characterized the development in tenth-century France was the large-scale replacement of royal power by local-aristocratic power: the aristocracy came to take the place of the king. This change in the power structure had nothing to do with any ecclesiological standpoint, but was conditioned by social and military circumstances. In practice, nevertheless, the effects were to be felt in the ecclesiastical field, especially in those regions in which the proprietary church system was firmly entrenched. Yet this tenth-century development was seen, from the ecclesiological angle, as a deviation

[8] Cf. *Patrologia Latina*, CXIX, 573 B, the letter which the clergy of Paris sent to the archbishop of Sens: "... *Aeneam, cuius praeconia praemisimus, concorditer omnes eligimus, Aeneam patrem, Aeneam pontificem optamus.*"

from the true canonical order of things. And as a result of the restoration of a somewhat more effective central government under the Capetians at the end of the century the awareness of the need of creating the bishops by the co-operation of king, clergy and people gradually increased, with the consequence that in the eleventh century the development began to take a course that was pre-portrayed in the ninth and early part of the tenth centuries. But other and no less grave issues came to the fore which impinged upon the free election of bishops: yet in themselves and in their consequences these issues assumed a complexion which had little in common with those which characterized the development in the ninth and tenth centuries.

Jean Leclercq

The General Chapters of the Cistercians, Cluny and the Dominicans

THE period when general chapters came into being also saw the appearance in the Church of cathedral chapters, and the birth and development in society of the phenomenon of corporations, manifested in various forms: charters and privileges granted to places, and especially to cities, with liberties and immunities from their lords, granting them the right to elect representatives and juries which could intervene in administration, justice and finance in order to achieve the mutual aid between them all which would encourage peace. Is there any correlation between these facts and what we know about general chapters? I offer three examples characteristic of three different traditions and three successive phases of the institution: the Cistercians, Cluny and the Dominican Order.

I. THE CISTERCIAN ORDER

Cluniac monks existed long before Cistercians, but the latter were the first to make general chapters a fundamental institution intended to function at regular intervals. In this they are representative of many new religious orders of monks and canons regular, which like themselves were set up from the beginning of the twelfth century on. The only difference is that they were earlier and more centrally organized than the others, and offer a typical example of a tendency which was extensive and powerful at this time. They did not have a general chapter at first. But a chapter was clearly established from the time of the drafting of

their fundamental document, the *Carta Caritatis*, which is attributed to the year 1119, though its text was later expanded and
modified.[1] The purpose of this "Cistercian Parliament", which
rapidly became a sovereign body, was to organize the exchange
of spiritual and material assistance between monasteries, with no
prejudice to the autonomy of each one, and to allow a kind of
control which avoided the arbitrary decisions of a single superior.[2]
Every year, at the date which was fixed in September, all the
abbots of the order—and they alone—were required under pain
of sanctions to go to Cîteaux, the mother house where the
assembly was held. During the chapter, and in respect of decisions
which had to be taken between two chapters, the abbot of Cîteaux
kept his dominant role. But since all the business could not be
dealt with in a few days by men who often arrived very tired, it
was found necessary from the middle of the twelfth century to
appoint "commissions" which prepared and continued the work,
and expert advisers called *diffinitores* because they drafted the
definitions, that is, the decisions. These decisions were voted upon
and adopted by majority vote, or, depending upon the subject,
by unanimous vote. But at Cîteaux, as everywhere else at that
period, there was a refusal to give an absolute value to the principle of the majority. In some cases, where opinions were divided,
the matter was left to the judgment "of the Abbot of Cîteaux
and those who are of wiser counsel", according to the somewhat
vague legal notion of the *senior pars*, which throughout the
Middle Ages led to so many quarrels and so many contested
elections.

The competence of the chapter extended to legislative and
judicial matters. It was also a court of justice which punished,
resolved disagreements and decided administrative issues. In
some cases, matters were submitted to the Holy See, or left to
the judgment of the arch-abbot. To resolve quarrels, the chapter

---

[1] Text in J. B. Van Damme, *Documenta pro Cisterciensis Ordinis his-
toriae ac juris studio* (Westmalle, 1959), 18, c. 4.

[2] J. B. Mahn, *L'Ordre cistercien et son gouvernement des origines au
milieu du XIIIe siècle (1098–1265)* (Paris, 1945), pp. 66–7, 197–216, 239–52;
G. Le Bras, *Institutions ecclesiastiques de la chrétienté médiévale. Pré-
liminaires*, Part I, Book I, in *Histoire générale de l'Église*, 12 (Paris, 1959),
pp. 486–90; D. Knowles, *From Pachomius to Ignatius. A Study in the
Constitutional History of the Religious Orders* (Oxford, 1966), pp. 24–8.

arbitrated in the conflict either directly or through the intermediary of commissions of abbots or judges delegate. Like any other institution, the Cistercian general chapter did not always function perfectly. There were sometimes intrigues and rivalries. It did not always arouse great interest on the part of those who should have taken part in it: absences not justified by the reasons permitted, but explicable by the difficulties of the journey, the lack of funds, or the resistance of communities, show a growing distaste for this kind of "obligatory ceremony". It nevertheless exercised a great influence, extending to the political affairs of Christendom. Throughout the twelfth and part of the thirteenth century, there were no regular international assemblies on this scale. It also influenced the organization of all orders of monks— ancient or modern—canons, hospitallers and the military orders. Centralization in the hands of the Abbot of Cîteaux was quite strong. Representation was solely by abbots, and other members of the communities were excluded. One can scarcely describe this as a democracy. But democracy was something which hardly existed in secular society to any great degree. At least the participation of the monasteries in the central government was further developed and better organized in the Cistercian Order than elsewhere.

II. Cluny

During the twelfth century, the bulk of the old monasteries of the traditional type—those later known as Benedictine—had only sporadic general chapters for minor decisions. Nevertheless, there were relationships of affiliation, and links of other kinds between many of them. But they did not feel the need for assemblies of this kind, which were only imposed upon them under Innocent III, by the fourth canon of the Fourth Lateran Council of 1215. Cluny is a clear example of their evolution in this respect.

Since 909 this monastery had existed as an independent abbey, and then as the head of an order which became very large, but whose structures remained very flexible. For almost two hundred years, this group of monasteries was governed for most of the time by four superiors whose periods of office as abbot were marked not only by their length but by a wisdom which led them to be regarded as saints. Their successors in the twelfth century were sometimes joined by what J. Houlier has called the "general chapter of an abbey", a kind of enlargement of the local chapter of the mother house, in which the priors of the daughter houses took part, as though they formed a single monastery existing in several places.[3] Twice, in 1132 and 1146, Pater the Venerable called a "universal chapter", in which he promulgated statutes which aroused hostility, but which were imposed by authority of Innocent II. Throughout the twelfth century, the Cluniac monks resisted the idea of having general chapters like those of all the new orders. It was not until 1200 that Hugh V, Abbot of Cluny, not only adopted the general chapter into the constitution, but invited four Cistercian abbots to take part in it. Nevertheless, it was necessary for Gregory IX to insist in 1231 that these chapters should be held. He was unwise enough to enforce the presence of Cistercian abbots, who had the task of teaching the Cluniac monks how to hold a chapter and of informing the Holy See every year of its results. The consequence of this measure was to strengthen the resistance of the Cluniac monks, certain of whom refused to come or to accept the decisions taken. Alexander IV in 1256 and Clement IV in 1265 dispensed them to some extent from this insulting supervision, which was not finally suppressed until 1289 by Nicholas IV. It was only from 1259 that there appeared, almost every year, the *Definitions of the General Chapter.*[4]

The chapter was held at Cluny every year after Easter. According to the provisions laid down by Gregory IX, those obliged to attend were the abbots and priors who were directly or indirectly dependent upon the Abbot of Cluny. But in fact the priors hardly ever came. Ordinary monks came only if they were required to be present for a case. By contrast to Cistercian practice, numerous excuses were sufficient to justify absence. The president was the Abbot of Cluny. The chapter began with the election of the

[3] J. Houlier, *Le chapître général jusqu'au moment du Grand Schisme. Origines, développement* (Paris, 1936), p. 28. Cf. also G. de Valous, *Le Monachisme clunisien des origines au XVᵉ siècle* (2nd ed., Paris, 1970), II, pp. 70–94; Mahn, *op. cit.*, pp. 245–50.
[4] Ed. G. Charvin, *Statuts, chapîtres généraux et visites de l'Ordre de Cluny*, Vols. 1–5 (Paris, 1965–1970).

visitors for the year and the *diffinitores* for the chapter. The latter were independent of the chairman. They were elected from amongst the superiors alone, and their number grew from four to fifteen. They were very powerful, and were actually the only active members of the meeting, the other members being no more than listeners reduced to a passive attitude almost without parallel. The visitors gave an account of their visits, reported the decisions and judgments they had given, and gave a check on the way the observance was kept. They also played the part of auditors: they verified the financial administration, which was often more difficult to maintain in order than the life of the rule. Like all the other monasteries, Cluny was subject to visitation and to the decisions of the *diffinitores*. But there were few conflicts between them and the Abbot of Cluny, and they were not of great importance. Not only did they maintain good relations, but the *diffinitores* often made use of the Abbot of Cluny to carry out their decisions, as chairman of the tribunal of the order and as an ambassador to princes and nobles and to the Holy See. Sometimes they even asked him to modify and improve their decisions. In turn, the Abbot of Cluny, assisted by his council, could change the visitors and appeal against the definitions; but he hardly ever made use of this right. Like the general chapter of the Cistercians, that of Cluny had an influence on politics; but this was mainly exercised by the Abbot of Cluny as intermediary. Thus the general chapter of Cluny seems to have been even less democratic than that of Cîteaux. The Cluniac order remained a kind of easy-going and moderate monarchy, with "a consultative assembly of heads of houses called to give their advice to help the Abbot of Cluny, whose task had become, by his own confession, too heavy".[5] Everything confirms the impression that there was agreement with what Innocent IV wrote to the Abbot of Cluny in 1246: "A people usually prospers under a single leader, while it is destined to ruin if it obeys a number."[6] The general chapter is an institution which was brought into full existence very slowly at Cluny, in spite of the pressure for it by a whole series of popes. This fact illustrates the persistence in this order

[5] De Valous, *op. cit.*, p. 37.
[6] Quoted *op. cit.*, p. 18.

of a spiritual and institutional tradition which was different from that of Cîteaux, but like Cîteaux pursued a respectable existence down the centuries until the French Revolution.

III. THE DOMINICAN ORDER

The Dominican Order is one of those which developed at the beginning of the thirteenth century and which are described as mendicant orders. The individual religious no longer belonged to an abbey but to a whole order, which was divided into provinces. Now in 1215, as we have seen, the Fourth Lateran Council laid down that the Benedictines and all who had already not done so should adopt the institution of general chapters. St Dominic shared in this movement. The text of the constitutions of his order which date from the years 1220–1228, and which are certainly inspired by him, contain a long section *On the General Chapter*.[7] This body functioned in a complex way. It did not differ fundamentally from the Cistercian and Cluniac chapters. Like them, it took place every year, its role was to govern, legislate, control and judge, and it carried out this task by the use of *diffinitores*. But its two original features were that the chapter elected the Master-General, who possessed executive power; and that not only the superiors but the ordinary religious took part in it. Thus those who were masters in the activity of preaching which is the aim of the whole institution, but held no position of authority, were represented in it. This structure reflected not the democratic intention of allowing the majority to prevail, or to give everyone the opportunity to put forward his opinion, but rather the need of assuring a balance between different institutional authorities, e.g., between the Master-General and the chapter, with the latter dominating. In the thirteenth century and later the Dominican constitutions were to influence many religious orders, the legislation of cities and even the constitution of a large country like England.[8]

[7] Text in P. Mandonnet, M. H. Vicaire, R. Ladner, *Saint Dominique. L'idée, l'homme et l'œuvre* (Paris, 1937), pp. 285–90; cf. also *ibid.*, p. 207 *et passim*; M. H. Vicaire, art. "Dominique (saint)", in *Dictionnaire d'histoire et de géographie ecclésiastique* 14 (1960), pp. 603–5; Mahn, *op. cit.*, pp. 250–1; Knowles, *op. cit.*, pp. 487–90.

[8] This E. Barker's thesis in *The Dominican Order and Convocation*.

It will be seen that it is anachronistic to speak of democratic government with regard to the three orders discussed here, except, perhaps, to an extent which must be carefully defined, among the Dominicans. It would be more accurate to talk of aristocratic government, particularly in the case of Cîteaux. As for Cluny, the general chapter was more of a council, in both senses of the word: a body which gives advice to authority, and a committee which draws up decrees. In these two orders at least, the wisest groups, the *sanior pars* whose view prevailed, could be the minority. And both amongst them and amongst the Dominicans the administrative techniques gave an important role to the *diffinitores*, who can be compared to commissions of experts or judges delegate. The conceptions of this period of the Middle Ages in constitutional law are very far from those worked out in the eighteenth and nineteenth centuries.

In short, in the twelfth and thirteenth centuries, Cîteaux, Cluny and the Dominican Order did not anticipate the later development of democratic institutions; they followed the tendencies of their own time. The Cluniac Order conformed only gradually, with a resistance due to the weight of an ancient tradition which was no doubt adequate to its own structure. But the Cistercians and the Dominicans had the virtue of giving to the forms of government which were being worked out almost everywhere at that period an exceptionally precise and solid structure, and in this way indicated one of the directions they might take. We would say nowadays that they were "pointers", or that they were "pilot schemes".

Was this organization of religious orders, desired by the popes, also the reflection of an evolution taking place in the government of the Church? Was it influenced by this evolution? Did it influence it? It seems that two spheres must be distinguished; that of the local churches and that of the Roman Church as a whole. From the first point of view, as we have said, a tendency towards a degree of representation and participation was common to religious orders, states and cities, and to cathedral chapters. The papacy did not oppose this tendency, which in any case it could

---

A Study of the Growth of Representation in the Church during the Thirteenth Century (Oxford, 1913).

not prevent. As for the government of the Catholic Church, to the extent that the general chapters encouraged the centralization of religious orders, they became a means of controlling them more effectively, with a view to permanently reforming them. This seems to be the reason why Rome tried to impose them. But to the extent to which they included a certain degree of representation and participation, was there any equivalent to them at the level of central power? The impression one has is that the evolution there was in the opposite direction.[9] It was actually in reaction against the degree of authoritarian centralization attained under Boniface VIII that there appeared for the first time in ecclesiology the idea that the government of the Church would be better if, instead of being purely monarchical, it was modified by a degree of democracy and aristocracy: "At that time Jean de Paris suggested that under a pope, in each province, several representatives of this province would be elected so that all to a certain extent would have a part in the government of the Church."[10] This formula was a bold one at the time, but was never brought to realization. Yet it corresponds to the practice of the Order of Preachers, to which this theologian belonged. The course of future development was as though the papacy had rejected, in the exercise of its own power, what it saw being introduced in ecclesiastical and lay society, and what it encouraged in the religious orders. The study of the reasons for such an attitude would no doubt require many careful distinctions, and would offer one more example of the gap that sometimes exists between ideas and facts.

Translated by R. A. Wilson

[9] This can be seen, for example, in what G. Le Bras, discussing the twelfth to fourteenth centuries, called "the concentration of powers", the "deployment of the primacy", "an extenuating monopoly", in *Institutions ecclésiastiques de la chrétienté médiévale*, Ière partie, livre I (Paris, 1959), pp. 305–14; also in *Histoire du droit et des institutions de l'Église en Occident*, I, *Prolégomènes* (Paris, 1955), pp. 140 *et passim*; and G. Le Bras, C. Lefebvre, J. Rimbaud, *ibid.*, VII, *L'âge classique, 1140–1378* (Paris, 1965), p. 588, and numerous references to the word "centralisation".

[10] *Johannes Quidort von Paris. Über königliche und päpstliche Gewalt (De regia potestate et papali)*, ed. Fritz Bleienstein (Stuttgart, 1969), 19, pp. 316–7.

Anton Weiler

Nicholas of Cusa on the Reform of the Church

ONE OF the most important aspects of the many suggestions that Nicholas of Cusa made regarding the reform of the Church and the Empire in his great treatise on "all-embracing agreement" (*De concordantia catholica*)[1] was the need to reactivate the consensus of subordinates in the Church over and against those in authority. In the fourteenth century, the Curia in Avignon had gained almost complete control over the appointment of bishops and canons, the payment of incomes, church taxes and benefices and prebends, even including those for university students. This centralization of power gave rise to many complaints a century later. A complaisance lower down in the Church had led to this practice becoming so firmly established that only a total mobilization of all existing forces in the local churches could offer any real hope of a restoration of good relations between the local clergy and people and their hierarchical leaders. Both Avignon and Rome had sent complete strangers as bishops to dioceses, had refused to recognize the appointment of elected bishops, or had transferred bishops after a short time to avoid causing unease because they had failed to understand the need above all for harmony between themselves and the local community.

A local problem was the starting-point for Nicholas of Cusa's treatise. He was present at the Council of Basle (1432) to plead the case of Ulrich of Manderscheid, who was the candidate of the

---

[1] Nicolai de Cusa, *Opera omnia* XIV, 2, *De Concordantia Catholica*, ed. G. Kallen (Hamburg, 1959–1965), 3 vols. (quoted as *DCC* with number).

nobility for the vacant archbishopric of Trèves, as against the candidate chosen by the cathedral chapter, Jacob of Sierck, who was himself a member of the chapter. The latter had appealed to the pope, who in turn put forward the bishop of Speyer, Rabanus of Helmstadt, as a candidate for the archbishopric of Trèves. Ulrich of Manderscheid was able to persuade the cathedral chapter to support him. He had then to match his strength against the man appointed by the pope.[2] If it could be proved that a bishop ought, according to reason, to divine and natural law and above all to the traditional practice of the Church, be able to rely on the consent of the members of his community and that this consent ought to be expressed at the election, then Manderscheid's case was won.[3]

Nicholas' argument, however, goes far beyond the purely local sphere to which it applied at the time. He saw very clearly that trust between the bishop and the Church, and the parish priest and the parish must be the foundation of a properly functioning community, and that this trust can be strengthened if the community is involved in the choice of its leader. He also realized that those in authority in the Church ought to recognize the sociological fact that the Church's legal enactments and provisions were made functionally valid by virtue of the consent given to them by those for whom they were intended as behavioural norms.

Nicholas' views about this reform in the Church and the Empire[4] are based on a study of the Church Fathers and the practice of the early councils. As Nicholas himself wrote elsewhere, reform was above all "going back to the first, primordial form".[5] All the same, he was also equally adept with rational and juridical arguments. He found in Aristotle's teaching about the

---

[2] M. Watanabe, *The Political Ideas of Nicholas of Cusa with Special Reference to his* De Concordantia Catholica (Geneva, 1963), p. 15.

[3] P. Sigmund, *Nicholas of Cusa and Medieval Political Thought* (Cambridge, Mass., 1963), p. 138.

[4] For the background to the proposed reform of the Empire, see A. G. Weiler, "Hervormingswil en normatief verleden in het denken van Nikolaas van Kues", in *Nederlands Archief voor Kerkgeschiedenis*, N.S. 52 (1972), which is shortly to be published.

[5] Quoted by E. Iserloh, *Reform der Kirche bei Nikolaus von Kues* (Wiesbaden, 1965), p. 8.

State, and in the provisions of Roman and Church law, a good
basis for convincing arguments and an excellent source of influence. The whole of his reasoning was sustained by a platoni-
cally based theology of the Spirit. It is, of course, not possible to
go into all these aspects of Nicholas' arguments here. We must
concentrate on his special contribution to the debate, which is,
I believe, to be found in the reactivation of what he regarded as
the practice of the early Church. He made an intensive study of
the early manuscripts, although he includes in his sources a
Pseudo-Isidorian forgery, which he apparently did not recognize
as false—this false decretal had been accepted uncritically from
earlier canonical collections and included in the *Decretum Gratiani*
of *c.* 1140, a document with which Nicholas was very well
acquainted.

Nicholas was above all concerned with the establishment of
a new practice in the Church. He recognized that all authority
had its origin in God, but he wanted to give the Christian community itself, as the vehicle which accepted and bore up that
authority, a new consciousness of itself as a body with an active
political part to play, if only through its elected representatives.
Above all, the members of the community were not simply to
be passively obedient—they had freely and if possible explicitly to
give their consent to the authority they had chosen and to the
rules they had evolved in accordance with those of the early
Church.

Unity was the basis of the Church's life and Nicholas was
therefore convinced that it was wrong to appoint a leader to a
community against the will of its members. Basing his arguments
on the sources of the Church's law and ancient practices, he insisted that all the members had, either explicitly or implicitly, to
appoint the leader of the community.[6] It was only in this way
that the differences in rank that had been introduced into the
Christian community for the sake of its well-being could be reconciled. The guarantee of its unity was respect for those placed

[6] *DCC* II, 233; source: among others, Pope Anicetus' letter to the bishops
of Gaul (Pseudo-Isidorian, based on a text of the Council of Carthage,
A.D. 429); Jaffé, No. 57; Hinschius, p. 120; *Decretum Gratiani*, D. 66 c. 1,
Archiepiscopus.

above in authority and love for those below.[7] This unity could be compared with the spiritual unity of marriage, which was also based on a mutual *consensus*.[8] This marriage, which Paul had used as an image of the Christian community, faithful to Christ as a bride is faithful to her bridegroom, came about by the *consensus* between those electing and those elected.[9]

The classical texts, *nullus invitis detur episcopus*[10] and *qui omnibus praeesse debet, ab omnibus eligatur*[11] led Cusanus eventually to make certain concrete proposals, which assured the members of the hierarchy of the *consensus* of those occupying a lower position in the Church. Priests in charge of parishes and cathedrals had to be elected, or at least appointed with the *consensus* of those with a lower status. Bishops were to be elected by the clergy with the *consensus* of the laity and archbishops had to be chosen by the bishops with the *consensus* of the clergy.

Nicholas not only quoted early Church texts in support of all these measures,[12] but insisted that the envoys of the Church provinces who were to assist the bishop of Rome (and who are now called cardinals) were to be elected by the archbishops of the provinces with the *consensus* of the bishops. Finally, the cardinals were to elect the pope—as far as possible with the *consensus* of the archbishops. Cusanus believed that the bishop of Rome would in this way have a permanent council representative

---

[7] *Ibid.*; source: the letter sent by Gregory I to the bishops of Gaul (A.D. 595); D. 89 c. 7 *ad hoc* and 45 c. 4 *licet.*

[8] DCC II, 164; source: Pope Evaristus' letter to all the bishops (Caput Pseudo-Isidore, c. 4); Minschius, p. 90; Jaffé, No. XX; c. 7 q. 1, c. 11 *Sicut vir* and many other texts in the same source.

[9] DCC II, 233; source as in note 8 above; also Innocent II's enactment at the Second Lateran Council (1139), c. 28; Mansi XXI, 533; D. 63 c. 35 *Obeuntibus.*

[10] DCC II, 232; source: Pope Celestine's letter to the bishops of Gaul (A.D. 428), epist. II, c. 5, in Leon. M. opp. III, 270; Jaffé No. 152; D. 61 c. 13 *Nullus invitis.*

[11] II, 232; source: see note 6 above.

[12] II, 164; source: with reference to the Council of Toledo (A.D. 633), a letter from Pope Leo to Bishop Rusticus of Narbonne (A.D. 458 or 459); Nicholas I's decree on the election of the pope (A.D. 1059); a letter from Anacletus to the bishops of Italy (Pseudo-Isidorian); a text of Isidore of Seville (?); a letter from Pope Gelasius to the bishops Philippus and Gerontius (A.D. 446–492) and the text of Anicetus already quoted.

of the whole Church. This would provide the best possible government of the Church.[13]

In Nicholas' opinion, this was also the best guarantee that Peter came from *petra*, Church. As Augustine had said, it was not that every aspect of the whole presidential power originated with the people, but that the dynamic and emotive aspects of that power originated—like the living soul, which came in its rationality from God—from the potential of matter.[14] The productive strength was voluntary subjection, something to which God had given his grace.[15] Augustine expressed this interplay in a single sentence: *ille gratia divina praefertur, qui communi consensu eligitur*.[16] All power is present *potentialiter* in the people, but a formative ray from above that is active in the *consensus* is required if this power is to be constituted *actu* in the leader. The people bear the image of God the Father, from whom the Son (= the clergy) proceeds. Nicholas of Cusa took this idea from Joachim of Fiore[17] and it is interesting to apply it to the sacral function of the Germanic people's assembly from which the monarchy arose, however much the *stirps regia* traced its origin back to the deity.[18] In this case, the people were regarded, not as ignorant and despicable (as they were by many other authors), but as sacred.[19]

The most interesting proposal that Nicholas makes, however, is the most distant from fifteenth-century practice—the suggestion that a council of elected cardinals, each one representing one province subject to the Roman Church, should be set up to

---

[13] *Ibid*.

[14] Augustine, *In Joannis evangelium tractatus*, 7, n. 14 (*PL*, 35, 1444).

[15] DCC II, 167.

[16] *Ibid*., with reference to a letter from Pope Gregory to the clergy of Milan (A.D. 593), c. 8 q. 2, c. 2 *Dilectissimi*; the text, however, is not found here.

[17] II, 108, *Exposito in Apocalypsim* (ed. Venetiis 1527), *Liber introductorius*, c. 24 p. 22vb.

[18] O. Höfler, "Der Sakralcharakter des germanischen Königstum", in *Das Königstum. Seine geistige und rechtliche Grundlagen. Vorträge und Forschungen* III (Lindau, 1956), pp. 99–100.

[19] For example, Conrad of Megenberg, *Tractatus contra Occam*, cap. 7: "*Genus ... laicorum est populus ignarus, qui potius doceri debet quam docere, potius duci quam ducere*"; see M. Wilks, *The Problem of Sovereignty in the Later Middle Ages* (Cambridge, 1963), pp. 53, 244, 287.

act as a day-to-day but permanent advisory body for the pope. For Nicholas, this was the first requisite for the reform of the Church, and he was convinced that the pope and these representatives of the Church provinces should together carry out the day-to-day government of the Church. Even though the archbishops might be in Rome, they ought not, Nicholas believed, be admitted to this papal council. Anyone *qui cursum Romanae curiae aliqualiter cognoscit* can at once understand the reasons for this proposal![20] In this instance too, Cusanus appealed to ancient practices in the Church. Even Boniface VIII can be called as a witness: on accepting office, he promised to carry out his functions with the consensus of the cardinals.[21] He was, however, enough of a realist to know that the first requisite for this reform was a reform of the college of cardinals, which had to be led back to its original representative function.[22]

Briefly summarized, Cusanus reasoned as follows. The pope was not permitted to take any action in the government of the Church, to change any canons or to make any new legal provisions, to alienate any ecclesiastical property or to replace anyone in authority in the Church without first obtaining the consensus of the members of this council. In precisely the same way, no bishop was allowed to take similar action without the consent of his college of priests.[23]

This corporative idea was also applied by Cusanus to every level in the Church. The bishop formed the diocesan Church with his chapter. The archbishop formed the provincial Church with his suffragans. The patriarch formed the patriarchal Church with his archbishops and the pope formed the Roman Church with the archbishop-representatives. All these leaders were, Nicholas believed, to exercise their sphere of government on the basis of the *consensus* given by their subordinates. This was because it was the harmony or unity and the implicit or explicit *consensus* expressed in the practice of or in the statements made

[20] DCC II, 164–6, 202.

[21] II, 189; *Professio Bonifatii VIII* (v.d. Hardt, *Magnum Concilium Constantiense*, I/586 ff.

[22] II, 132; see also 191.

[23] II, 191–3; source: an enactment of the Council of Carthage (A.D. 419) and the Fourth Council of Toledo (A.D. 633); c. 12 q. 2, c. 51 *Placuit and* 58 *Episcopus*.

by those who represented the others in the Church which bound all the constitutions together.[24]

This text leads us on to one last point. We have already seen that, in Nicholas' opinion, this *consensus* operated at two levels —the one elected to an authoritative position in the Church carried out his duties in co-operation with the elected representatives of the lower hierarchical structures. Nicholas, however, also pointed out a third level at which this *consensus* functioned constitutively, and was necessary if authoritative decisions were to be actively accepted by those in a subordinate position in the Church. In this context, he used the traditional terms *"acceptatio"*, *"receptio"* and *"usus"*.[25]

He did not deny that the authorities had the power to make various legal enactments and provisions, but emphasized his conviction that the firmest foundation of all canons was *concordantia*, that any council was constituted by virtue of *consensus*, and that there was no council where there was *dissensio*. If, then, the statutes of the Church were to have the force of law, it was absolutely necessary to have *consensum per usum et acceptationem*. The statutes of the African Church in Gaul would, for example, have had no legal validity at all, if Charlemagne had not introduced them into Gaul through the collection of canons of Dionyso-Hadrian and Gaul had not accepted them as such.[26] This acceptance was necessary, since every law must, from the sociological point of view, accord with the country, the place and the time.[27]

According to Augustine, only what is contained in Scripture, in episcopal enactments made in councils, and in the practice of the universal Church can be regarded as binding.[28] The same applies to the provisions of the bishop of Rome, although these cease to be legally binding in the case of *non usum*.[29] Even if the

---

[24] DCC II, 132.   [25] II, 131.

[26] II, 101–102; source: Anselm of Lucca (1086), *Collectio canonum, in prooem.*

[27] II, 103, 130; source: Isidore, *Liber Etymologiarum*, V 21; D. 4 c. 2 *Erit autem*.

[28] II, 103; Augustine, *Ad inquisitiones Januarii*; Epist. 55 c. 12, *Omnia talia*.

[29] *Ibid.*; source: Gratian's commentary on D. 4 c. 4: *"Leges instituuntur, cum promulgantur, firmantur, cum moribus utentium approbantur."* The

pope is in the habit of making decisions entirely on his own, this practice does not apply in opposition to divine and natural law, according to which laws are approved by the conduct of those who use them.[30] If the pope makes an enactment and it is accepted as part of the Church's practice, the enactment is regarded as *synodice*. The practice of the universal Church is equated with the status of the bishops in council and a synodal decision includes *acceptatio* and *confirmatio*.[31] The *consensus* of the Church with regard to a papal decision can equally well be expressed by silence. The bishops of Rome have, for example, frequently used reservations in the appointment of bishops through the silent consent of the whole Church, and the bishops given by them have not been refused. In such cases, silence has clearly indicated a *consensus* and this has been sufficient legal ground for those who have been appointed in this way.[32] This does not, however, mean that the right of the Church to elect bishops is total or that it can be annulled. A certain unease arose at the time when Cusanus was writing because these reservations were used excessively and Cusanus insisted that the pope could not continue in this way unless he had explicitly been allowed to do so by a council: *"papa enim invitis episcopum dare non potest"*.[33]

Clearly, the origin of authority in the Church had to be discussed rationally from the historical and the theological points of view. In connection with the texts mentioned here, Nicholas agreed with many exegetes that Peter had been appointed in accordance with the will of the apostles, in the sense that he had been chosen by Christ before his resurrection, but had been confirmed in that appointment by the apostles, over whom he was

---

opposite, however, is also true—the decision taken by Pope Telesphorus (Pseudo-Isidorian) concerning the fasting of the clergy, which was not approved by the practice of those who used this law, did not make those who transgressed against it guilty. The same argument is found in the commentary *Hec etsi* D. 4 c. 6. 30. II, 109.

[30] DCC II, 109.

[31] II, 108; the text of Nicholas of Cusa refers to Augustine's pronouncement (see note 28); see also II, 106.

[32] II, 239, with reference to the *Glossa antiqua* as D. 63 c. 12.

[33] II, 238, 240, with reference to Anacletus' letter to the bishops of Italy (Pseudo-Isidorian!), in which we read: *"Ceteri vero apostoli cum eodem (Petro) pari consortio honorem et potestatem acceperunt, ipsumque principem eorum esse voluerunt. . . ."* D. 21 c. 2 *In novo.*

to preside, after the resurrection.[34] However interesting this question may be, I am prevented by lack of space from going into it here.

Cusanus believed that it was essential to restore the full procedure of election if the Church was to be reformed effectively. Three requisites for this, in the case of the appointment of bishops, were election by the clergy, the *consensus* of the people and the judgment of the archbishop.[35] If these conditions were fulfilled, an authority that was fully accepted in practice would be established and its enactments would be carried out. There were also, in Cusanus' view, three requisites if the enactments and provisions made by this authority were to be accepted as legally valid—power in the one carrying them out, the approval of the enactments in the practice of the Church and their publication.[36] If harmony and unity were to be established in the Church, *consensus* and *acceptatio* had to be active forces with regard to authority. Pope Hormisdas' frequently quoted pronouncement, "God is where consensus exists without wickedness",[37] clearly permeated Nicholas of Cusa's whole argument about "all-embracing agreement" in the Church.

The thought of Thomas Aquinas has for a very long time dominated the theology of the Church. It would seem that the time may have come to allow the ideas of Nicholas of Cusa, which provide us with an excellent insight into the way in which the early Church was organized, to inspire our thinking about the practical reform of the Church today.

Translated by David Smith

[34] DCC II, 240, where he quotes and agrees with Archidiaconus (=Guido de Baysio), following John de Deo; see the annotation of Kallen, 240, 10–14.
[35] II, 237.   [36] II, 105.
[37] II, 104, 167; Hormidas' letter to the bishops of Spain; Jaffé, 787; *PL* 63, 424, Hinschius, p. 690.

Antony Black

The Influence of the Conception of Absolute Monarchy upon the Understanding and Practice of Papal Authority

ABSOLUTE monarchy, in the sense in which it can be said to have influenced the papacy, is probably as old as civilization, almost as old as mankind. The period of modern European history often called "the age of absolute monarchy" (the sixteenth to eighteenth centuries) witnessed a rejuvenation and development of ancient ideas of which the papacy was one important vehicle. There can be no question of any significant influence of the ideas of absolute monarchy in this specific historical sense upon the papacy, since papal ideas on the subject were already fully developed and indeed more explicit and complete than the divine-right or absolute theories of secular monarchy in modern Europe ever were. By this time, the influence was almost entirely in the other direction. There was, indeed, a milieu of thought and feeling favourable to absolute monarchy in the later fifteenth and sixteenth centuries, from which the papacy for a time benefited marginally. But the main impact of absolutist ideas on the papacy was of a much earlier date.

The central notion was that of legal sovereignty, which the papacy appropriated from Roman-imperial legal thought in the post-Constantinian era. According to this, the Roman see held the *principatus ecclesiae* in the legal sense that its verdict on an ecclesial dispute was final: it was the supreme court. That there was such a supreme court was thought to be implicit in the Petrine and apostolic commission, which gave power of binding and loosing from sin to specific individuals; that it should be the pope's court was argued from the familiar gospel texts about

Peter. The contribution of the Roman-imperial model here was merely to spell out the meaning in judicial terms.[1] During the later Middle Ages, this was further developed into a general legal and political theory, to the effect that this finality or sovereignty must be a feature of any rational, workable, legal or political system.[2]

But other attributes of the Roman emperor were attached to this central notion: first of all his legislative authority; Gregory VII (1075) was the first pope to claim unequivocally the power to make and unmake ecclesial laws, and this was later justified by the Roman-legal text that the decision of the prince has the force of law.[3] In other words, what occurred, on this and similar questions, throughout the period between Constantine and Luther, was a gradual extension of the imperial analogy, so that in the end one was faced with the phenomenon of a body of doctrine, "medieval papalism", in which the imperial analogy played a determining, as well as an illustrative, role. Again, it was claimed that the pope, as *princeps ecclesiae*, was *"legibus solutus"*, just like the emperor; this too came to be argued on grounds of political expediency, it being seen as a necessary feature of any workable legal system that the head must be himself free from legal obligation; otherwise he is not the true head and you are without a final judicial court.[4] This analogy was linked to that between the papacy and kingship, which derived from biblical references to the Church as "the kingdom of heaven" and as "a royal priesthood".

But the revolution in political thought achieved by the papacy in medieval Europe was due to the appropriation of a different imperial title which corresponded remarkably closely to the papacy's (or any ecclesial authority's) theologically defined status. This was the representation of God on earth. This had been a traditional claim of sacerdotal monarchy from very early times in the civilizations of the Near East; it had been appropriated by

[1] W. Ullmann, *The Growth of Papal Government in the Middle Ages* (3rd ed.: London, 1965), esp. pp. 9–20.
[2] M. J. Wilks, *The Problem of Sovereignty in the Later Middle Ages* (Cambridge, 1965), pp. 152–3, 158–9.
[3] *Das Register Gregors VII*, ed. E. Caspar (Berlin, 1955), p. 203.
[4] A. J. Black, *Monarchy and Community* (Cambridge, 1970), pp. 73-8.

the Roman empire. It is well known how certain Christian writers ascribed this role even to pagan emperors; and it was a dominant theme in European divine-right theory centuries later. But while in East Rome and its off-shoots Christian theology generally maintained this view of the emperor, the papacy in the West appropriated this claim for itself. What was intended was perhaps primarily a rationalization in contemporary language of the notion of ecclesial authority; but once again the analogy with the old imperial position had further repercussions. In the absence of any clear distinction between Church and State, and on the assumption that "all power is from God", the papacy claimed authority as God's representative over secular rulers, both as Christians and as holding important posts within the *republica christiana*. In the claim that the pope was "king of kings", the divine analogy was clearly intended to mean that all other rulers were in some sense his subordinates, a relationship fully realized in the cases where the pope entered into feudal contracts with kings as his vassals. In practical terms, it meant that the pope could not only excommunicate but actually depose a ruler, either *"ratione peccati"* or because he was "useless", and that he could even preside over the appointment of a successor. Thomas Aquinas, who in general distinguished very carefully between ecclesial and temporal power, declared that both resided in the pope;[5] the crusades were an example of his active leadership of Christendom in a cause that was seen as both spiritual and secular.

Just as, during the High Middle Ages, the papacy claimed and occasionally exercised power in the temporal sphere (particularly in imperial territories), so during the later Middle Ages the secular rulers often claimed and exercised power over church benefices as part of the process of centralization and territorial integration. Vis-à-vis other ecclesial authorities in the West, the papacy had by the fourteenth century achieved a high degree of centralization and bureaucratic control; indeed the papal bureaucratic machine, as well as its centralizing ideology, provided something of a model for secular states. When this was challenged during the Great Schism and the Conciliar Movement, the papacy gravi-

[5] *Comm. in IV Sent.*, d. 44, q. 3, a. 4.

tated towards a compromise with its former rivals for secular power, with whom it made concordats agreeing to a share for both pope and king over benefices.[6] This realignment accompanied a significant shift in papal political thought. The monarchical ideology previously worked out for the papacy, and fully displayed in the works of such writers as Augustine of Ancona and his fifteenth-century imitator St Antonino of Florence, was now presented as corresponding to the entire natural-political order, thus postulating in every state a similar monarchical regime. It was now that a single set of governmental ideas was worked out, applicable to papacy or royalty.[7]

The philosophical basis for this appears to have been the Christian neo-Platonism of Pseudo-Denis, which was used to demonstrate the existence of a universal natural order with God at its head, and created beings arranged in a "hierarchy" below; it was stated that this held good for every society, human as well as divine, secular as well as ecclesial. The ruler was seen as occupying in his society the place of God in the universe—a role which he could hardly live up to organizationally, let alone ethically—so that all subordinate offices were not only subject to his nomination but were in their essence dependent upon his authority, could be changed at will, and bypassed whenever he wished. This theory was largely responsible for the phrase "plenitude of power" (adopted by the papacy in earlier times and now borrowed by secular rulers from Louis IX to Alfonso V of Aragon), which was another way of saying that all legitimate authority ultimately stemmed from the head, by his express or tacit consent. It was also a way of rationalizing the identification of ruler with community, in the sense that he wielded in law and polity the powers ascribed to the community as a whole, because the "hierarch" is thought to contain within himself, "implicitly" at least, all the powers delegated to those below him; thus he "represents" the community *ex natura rei*, because its powers are "absorbed" in him.[8] (There is an interesting similarity between this view and

[6] W. Bertrams, *Der neutzeitliche Staatsgedanke und die Konkordate des ausgehenden Mittelalters* (Rome, 1950).

[7] K. Eckermann, *Studien zur Geschichte des monarchischen Gedankens im 15 Jahrhundert* (Berlin, 1933).

[8] O. Gierke (trans. Maitland), *Political Theories of the Middle Ages*

Hegel's doctrine of "the State", no doubt due to their common idealist origin.) This was true "absolutism", thoroughly Platonic in conception, and of course it ran counter both to ecclesial theory and to secular reality at many points. It left no place, first, for the independent status of either bishops or the episcopate as such;[9] and it assumed that the sovereign was *de facto* as well as *de iure* omnipotent.

During the later Middle Ages the emperor and other secular rulers busily added certain features of papal derivation, such as the neo-Platonic formulas, to their own statements of their status as sovereigns. A few writers explicitly referred to the papacy as a precedent for monarchical sovereignty.[10] Supporters of the papacy, meanwhile, worked up the various secular analogies into a statement of monarchical theory that purported to rest upon natural-political as well as theological principles, and which was therefore both modelled upon and applicable to secular kingdoms. Juan de Torquemada's *Summa de Ecclesia* (1449) suggests that what gave overwhelming logic to such a theory was the assumption of a neo-Platonic world-view.[11] Aeneas Piccolomini, whose career straddled the ecclesial and secular spheres of government, shows that the Empire was now reversing the process of the early Middle Ages, by using the papal analogy to buttress its own claims.[12]

This was accompanied by a shift in papal temporal claims; supporters of the papacy, from Torquemada to Bellarmine, emphasized the "indirect" nature of papal temporal power,[13] and Pius II urged a crusade on humanitarian as well as religious grounds, begging secular rulers to support him since on this issue "we cannot so much command as ask". The one secular aim of

---

(Cambridge, 1900), pp. 62-3 (*Das deutsche Genossenschaftsrecht*, III: Berlin, 1881).

[9] Cf. Suarez on the human origin of the *episcopalis iurisdictio* in *Tract. de legibus*, IV, vi, 14.

[10] Black, *op. cit.*, pp. 80-4.

[11] *Ibid.*, pp. 57-62.

[12] A. S. Piccolomini, *De ortu et auct. Romani imperii*, c. 11, 16, 18, 23, 24. Cf. B. Widmer, *Enea Silvio Piccolomini* (Basle, 1963), pp. 130 ff.

[13] P. Theeuws, "Jean de Turrecremata. Les relations entre l'église et le pouvoir civil . . . ", in *Receuil de trav. d'hist. et de philol.*, 3 xviii (Louvain, 1943), pp. 138-78. J. Gemmel, "Die Lehre d. Kard. Bellarmins ueber Kirche u. Staat", in *Scholastik* 5 (1930), pp. 357-79.

the papacy which continued to be voiced was that of international peace.

This, then, is the connection between absolute monarchy as a phenomenon of modern European history and the papacy. The arrival of a developed monarchical theory as the generally accepted political norm for Europe—Lutheran and Catholic—owed something both to the world-view of Christian neo-Platonism and to the papal precedent, both of which helped to establish the legitimacy of absolute monarchy as a divinely ordained pattern.[14] Bodin, for example, remarked that it was the canonist-pope Innocent IV who had "most clearly" understood the meaning of sovereignty, and referred to "the canonists" as supporting his view of the legal irresponsibility of a sovereign.[15] More than that, he could have found in Torquemada a defence of monarchical sovereignty in rational-utilitarian terms, as necessary for the unity of society and the effectiveness of government, such as he himself put forward.

That monarchy for men of the sixteenth century was clearly to be distinguished from despotism or tyranny, in that it consisted in the rule of one man for the good and by the consent of the governed, must also owe much to the general prevalence of Christian ethical ideas. A political idealist such as Erasmus regarded monarchy as the best form of government because it imitated the divine order of the cosmos, and also because it was held to be essential to the ruler-ruled relationship that the ruler should be free from legal coercion; the analogy with a father, a general was always to hand. Hence Erasmus bids the king behave justly and even democratically, be approachable by all, and consult his subjects' interests and views; but, like Bodin after him, he thinks that to make constitutional government legally binding upon the monarch would be a contradiction in terms.[16] His relationship with his subjects was for life what the relationship between a modern government and its people is between elections. If he is *"legibus solutus"*, he must be all the more morally and

[14] Cf. G. R. Elton's introduction to J. N. Figgis, *The Divine Right of Kings* (Harper Torchbook ed.: New York, 1965).
[15] J. Bodin, *Les six livres de la République*, I, 8.
[16] D. Erasmus, "Institutio principis christiani", in *id.*, *Opera Omnia* (Lugduni Bat. 1703), pp. 560–611, esp. 66, 576–7.

legally irreproachable. In the last resort, the personal allegiance of subjects to monarch was seen as a final sanction against civil war; but, if he was a monarch and not a tyrant, it must be willing allegiance, loyalty, *"fides"*. This political theory was obviously not, as the works of Bodin demonstrate, logically satisfying or of lasting validity; it was to many emotionally pleasing, and it met certain contemporary needs—not unlike "one-party" rule in developing countries today; and, like them, it provided a focal point for national unity and social identity.

Yet, at the very time when secular thought was borrowing ecclesial precedents, ecclesiology itself was undergoing a transformation, a rejuvenation, hastened though not begun by the Reformation. From the early fifteenth century, we begin to hear that ecclesiology has become warped by the secular analogy, imported by canonists who have not given sufficient weight to the sources of revelation; it is the domain of theology, not of canon law. We hear this both from Conciliarists like van der Velde and Segovia, and from Papalists like Institoris and Cajetan. St Bernard's theological morality of ecclesial government, based on Matthew 20. 25–8, is given more prominence even by pro-papal as well as conciliar writers. This text, of course, destroyed the secular analogy at root: "You know that among the pagans the rulers lord it over them and their great men make their authority felt. This is not to happen among you...."

Even in the heyday of the secular-monarchical analogy in the Church, the Council of Florence had given it a modest role, referring only to Peter as *"princeps apostolorum"* and the description of the pope's function as one of "ruling and governing" came after and alongside the description of it as "pasturing".[17] From the late fifteenth century, the analogy with secular monarchy seems to play an altogether less important role, as one among many ways of regarding church government. The Conciliarist Segovia had not been untypical in insisting that church government could not be modelled on any given secular prototype; it was *sui generis*.[18] Cajetan, in controversy, might insist that, of the three possible forms of government, Christ had de-

---

[17] Denzinger, *Enchiridion*, ed. 30, 253.
[18] Juan de Segovia, *Hist. gest. Basil. conc.*, bk. XVII, c. lix–lx, in *Mon. conc. gen. sec. 15*, III, 934, 937–8.

liberately chosen the monarchical for the Church;[19] but apart
from that he shows little interest in secular precedent, and indeed
in one notable passage very clearly delineates the meaning of
"principatus" for ecclesial government: *"etsi 'pascere non significat principari'* (his opponents' view), *significat tamen Christi
oves regere, in quo clauditur principari ... trahit secum principari, sicut trahit secum requirere, reducere, alligare, consolidare
et sanare...."*[20] In other words, it is one possible description of
a process which is essentially *sui generis.*

Gerson, and following him Denis Rickel "the Carthusian",
agree that the Church is a monarchy, but insist that this means
the best kind of monarchy, which is "mixed monarchy", i.e., it
includes "aristocratic" and "democratic" elements.[21] This view
is repeated, with the caution that monarchy applies at the top of
the ecclesial structure, by Bellarmine, who also insists that there
can be no such thing as "absolute" or "free" monarchy in the
Church (except for that of Christ) but only *"talis qualis esse potest
ministrorum et dispensatorum".*[22] The *Dictionnaire de Théologie
Catholique* expresses an identical view.[23]

The Council of Trent confined itself to asserting that there is
in the Church *"hierarchiam ex divina ordinatione institutam,
quae constat ex episcopis, presbyteris et ministris".*[24] Hence the
age of absolutism saw no new addition to the earlier borrowing
of secular monarchical concepts by the papacy, but rather, it
seems, a muting of the earlier strident claims. This was no doubt
partly due to the withdrawal of the papacy's temporal claims,
and to a new awareness of the distinction between ecclesial and
secular affairs, and so between the two models of government,
forced upon the Catholic Church partly by the Reformation
(which finally dissolved the *respublica christiana*), and partly by

[19] Thomas de Vio (Cajetan), *De comp. auct. papae et conc.,* i, in Roca-
berti, *Bibl. max. pontif.,* XIX. Edizione critica dell'opera di Caietano,
curata da J. V. Pollet (Rome, 1936).
[20] *Id., De divina instit. pontificatus* (1521), xi, ed. F. Lauchet (*Corpus
Catholicorum,* x) (Münster, 1925), p. 63.
[21] J. Gerson, *Opera Omnia,* ed. L. Dupin (Antwerp, 1706), I, p. 918 and
II, p. 279. D. Rickel, *Opera Omnia* (Tournai, 1908), XXXVI, pp. 624-5.
[22] R. Bellarmine, *Opera Omnia* (Paris, 1870), Vol. I, pp. 461 ff.
[23] *DTC,* VI, pp. 1532 ff.
[24] Denzinger, *ed. cit.,* p. 338.

the emergence of strong, unified and ambitious states all over Europe, but also by a return to the theological sources themselves. Bossuet, for instance, though a celebrated advocate of secular absolutism, has (as one would expect of a Gallican theologian) no place for it in the Church; he repeats the conciliar contention that the pope is "supreme in the Church, but not superior to the whole Church even when assembled".[25] Elsewhere he says, "the Roman Church is the mother of the churches, but not an imperious mistress; and you [the pope] are not the lord of the bishops but one of them"; and, after citing St Bernard, *"il y a toujours ... quelque chose de doux et fraternelle dans le gouvernement de l'église".*[26]

The relationship between papacy and absolute monarchy, then, goes back to the fourth century; the influence of the latter upon the former was a medieval phenomenon, and the modern period witnesses some degree of influence the other way round, but on the whole a parting of the ways. The lasting effect on ecclesiology was the description of the Church as a "monarchy". In substance, it meant that there was a process for making final decisions in the Church, by means of a legal sovereign; it seems also to have meant that final responsibility for doing so devolves upon one man, the successor of Peter. Thus, the First Vatican Council uses the old Roman-law terms *princeps* and *principatum* in describing the pope: *"princeps pastorum et pastor magnus ... super omnes alias ordinarie potestatis obtinere principatum".*[27]

In conclusion, it may be worth remarking that there must always be a distinction between legal sovereignty, in the sense of a court of final appeal—which is the basis of the concept of *principatus*—and other meanings of "sovereignty" which became confused with this in absolutist theory. Just because a certain court makes final decisions does not necessarily mean that it can legislate or determine political policy. Furthermore, no political organ can in practice—as was claimed in neo-Platonic political thought—stand outside the social system in which it operates. It must always take into consideration what is possible and acceptable, in particular public opinion, if it wishes to be effective

[25] Bossuet, *Œuvres complètes* (Paris, 1828), XLIII, p. 295.
[26] *Op. cit.*, VI, p. 115.
[27] Denzinger, *ed. cit.*, pp. 502-3.

and to survive. Even Bodin, for example, was forced to admit that a monarch who changed the *leges imperii* (constitutional laws of the realm) was performing a legally invalid act, which would have to be disregarded as soon as he died. Similarly, nearly all those medieval thinkers who painted the pope as an absolute monarch also envisaged certain circumstances (contradicting established doctrine, abolishing a sacrament or the episcopate) in which he might be deposed or excommunicated, not by a superior human authority, but *"ipso facto"* or *"ipso iure"*; that is, by the very nature of the act. We may interpret this as meaning that by a certain action he might contradict the very *raison d'être* of his own supremacy, which was *"in beato Petro"* and for the purpose of expounding Christian doctrine, pasturing the Christian people, and so on. In this case he would be like a prime minister who summed up a cabinet decision by saying "I am going to stand on my head", or a parliament which decreed that wheat should be grown on a mountain peak. This is to say, any position of sovereignty presupposes a certain "language game", and it presupposes the normal bounds of rationality. The problem with sovereignty is that these cannot altogether be defined in advance, in the abstract (so far as they can be, they are, in the form of constitutional law or the defined ecclesial tradition); future decisions have to be left open, and they have to be put in the hands of defined individuals. But no one would suggest that this gives those individuals "absolute" power in the sense that they can do what they like, only in the special sense that they are legally irresponsible. There are always, in any society, extra-legal sanctions, which are *ex hypothesi* impossible to define in advance, but which everybody, if they reflect, knows to exist.

Enrique Dussel

The Appointment of Bishops in the First Century of "Patronage" in Latin America (1504–1620)

ALTHOUGH general histories of the Church do not yet take it into account, Latin America (which now comprises thirty per cent of the world's Catholic population, a figure which will rise to over fifty per cent by the end of the century) underwent a development of its own from the fifteenth century. It was the only "colonial Christendom", dependent originally—from 1492—on Spain and Europe, and under the religious aegis of Latin (since 485, when the Pope came to occupy virtually the position of Roman Emperor) or Byzantine (since the inauguration of the Constantinian era in 330) Christendom.

Since then, the Latin-American episcopate has played an ever-increasing part in the affairs of the universal Church. It sent six hundred and one bishops to Vatican II, as opposed to only sixty-five to Vatican I, and none to Trent—thanks to the obstacles set up by Spanish "patronage", although several bishops, such as Zumárraga of Mexico and Vasco de Quiroga of Mechoacan, made every effort to get there.[1] By chance, one got to the Lateran Council in 1517, to one session only: this was Don Alejandro de Geraldini, bishop of Santo Domingo.

[1] For a general description of the history of the Church in Latin America, cf. Dussel, *Hipótesis para una historia de las Iglesia en América Latina* (Barcelona, 1967), revised and augmented as *América Latina en la historia de la salvación* (Barcelona, 1972). For the episcopate, cf. the bibliography in Dussel, *Les évêques hispano-américains, défenseurs et évangélisateurs de l'indien, 1504-1620* (Wiesbaden, 1970), pp. 1-61.

I. The Latin-American Episcopate in the Sixteenth Century

Despite its early unimportance on the European scene, in Latin America the episcopate soon produced a pastoral and evangelizing movement of a conciliar character. A series of important provincial councils, starting with Lima in 1552 and continuing till 1774 in the colonial era, led to the first continental council of the Catholic Church, the first Plenary Council of Latin America, held in Rome in 1899. Their conclusions were applied by numerous diocesan synods, well in tune with regional needs. I have been able to trace seventy-eight of these between 1536 and 1636. This conciliar tradition made possible the foundation of the Council of the Latin American Episcopate, CELAM, in 1955, and led to the Medellín conference of 1968.

In the sixteenth century, the episcopate, though elected under the "patronage system", represented the heart of the cultural, and of course the religious, life of the colonies. The bishops were responsible for founding colleges and universities, for installing printing presses, organizing missions, and lending their paternally authoritative weight to every sort of involvement in the day-to-day economic, social, political and military life of the colonies.

Far more important on the world scene was the fact that from 1544 to 1568 there was a generation of bishops who placed the whole authority of the ecclesial institution behind the defence of the Indians, the "protectorate". There were several outstanding figures involved: Zumárraga founded the first Indian seminary, in Tlaltelolco: Vasco de Quiroga organized thousands of Indians into a hundred and fifty communities, sharing their possessions in common, in the first experiments in what were to become known later as the "reductions"; in Lima, St Toribio of Mogrovejo gave outstanding witness of heroic virtue as a "reformed" pastor—"reformed" in the sense that the Latin American episcopate grew up in the shadow of the reforms instituted by Cardinal Cisneros: their poverty was as exemplary as their personal life (I have not been able to find a single accusation on this score against any of the hundred and fifty-seven bishops resident between 1504 and 1620).

Even more remarkable was the work of Bartolomé de las

Casas, bishop of Chiapas, who was expelled from his diocese by his Spanish flock for his defence of the Indians after only a few months' residence; he was more fortunate than Antonio de Valdivieso, who died a martyr's death for his defence of the Indians, assassinated by the Governor of Nicaragua; or than Pablo de Torres, bishop of Panama, who was sent back to Spain in chains for the same reason; or Juan del Valle, bishop of Popayán, who having done all he could for his Indians went to the Audience of Santa Fe in Bogotá and to the Council of the Indies in Spain, and when not listened to in either place set out to plead his case at the Council of Trent, but died in the South of France before reaching it; or Agustín de la Coruña, arrested in his own cathedral and held captive for five years because his Spanish flock could not stand his continual efforts on behalf of the Indians.

All this constitutes a vitally important piece of social history, whose relevance is not lost on developing nations today. Bartolomé de las Casas' prophetic book *The Destruction of the Indies* is an example to many dependent and oppressed peoples in their struggle to free themselves from colonialism or neo-colonialism.

II. SPANISH "PATRONAGE" IN AMERICA IN THE SIXTEENTH CENTURY

In Spain and Portugal, the absolutist policies of their monarchs and the weakness of Rome, which needed Iberian support in Italy and the rest of Europe, led to an increasing identification of the Church with the Crown. First Portugal obtained from Rome *possessio* of the lands conquered from the Saracens in North Africa.[2] Soon after, Spain acquired the same *jus patronatus* guaranteeing her full powers in the Canary Islands (1418). The "Catholic monarchs", Fernando and Isabel, obtained the Bulls *Provisionis nostrae* and *Dum ad illam* (1486) for organizing the final crusade against the kingdom of Granada, which gave the Crown all sorts of powers over the churches that would be set up in Arab lands. This is why the conquest of Granada (1492) and

---

[2] *Aeterni Regis* of 8 January 1455. *Bullarum Patronatus Portugalliae Regnum* (Lisbon, 1868), Vol. I, p. 49.

the "patronage" exercised there, was the precursor of the patronage in the Church in America, which Columbus discovered in the same year. Armed with the further Bulls *Inter coetera* and *Eximiae devotionis* (1493), Fernando of Aragón began organizing what was to become known as the "patronage" system in Latin America, which gave him the right to "present" bishops, set the boundaries of dioceses and parishes, send out religious and missionaries, receive Church tithes, supervise synods and councils, delegate these powers to the civil authorities, and so on.

In the "Fernandine period" (1504–1516), from the moment Rome named the first three bishops for America, on 15 November 1504, the king showed how he intended to exercise his rights of "patronage": he demanded and succeeded in having confirmed by the Bull *Universalis Ecclesiae* of 28 July 1508, that these appointments be annulled on the grounds that the candidates had not been chosen or appointed by the king, nor had he decided the Sees or the boundaries of the new bishoprics. Once the three candidates had been settled, the dioceses of Santo Domingo, Concepción de la Vega and Puerto Rico were founded at the Consistory of 8–13 November 1511. The first three bishops, Garciá de Padilla, Alonso Manso and Pedro Suarez de Deza, met the king in May 1512 to establish the "Capitulation of Burgos" by which they explicitly pledged themselves to defence of royal "patronage". The "executive orders"[3] were eventually handed to them on 27 December 1512.

There was then a "transitional period" from 1516 to 1524, beginning in the regency of Cisneros, during which the dioceses of Santiago de Cuba and Carolense were founded, in 1517 and 1519 respectively, bringing the total to six, as Santa María la Antigua in Panama had also been founded at the end of the Fernandine period, in 1513.

The "patronage" system took on its definitive form with the establishment of the Council of the Indies in 1524. This had been planned by a team led by Cardinal Loaysa in Valladolid the previous year. The Council elaborated a whole juridical structure

---

[3] "Executive orders" was the term given to the ensemble of "Royal Charters" that enabled the Bulls of the Roman Consistory to be "executed" or "carried out".

that became known as the *Laws of the Indies*, made up of a series of Royal Charters emanating from the throne—not collected into volume form till 1681, though they were worked out during the sixteenth century. They include the most important definitions of the king's rights of patronage: "The right of ecclesiastical patronage belongs to us throughout the whole state of the Indies" (Bk. I, Tit. VI), so that "the archbishoprics, bishoprics and abbeys of our Indies will be supplied through presentations made by us to our very Holy Father" (*ibid.*).

By 1620 the Council had founded twenty-nine bishoprics in America, the first being Mexico, established at the Consistory of 2 September 1530, and the last, Durango, on 28 September 1620.

Candidates for pastoral functions in America presented themselves continually to the Council in Spain. The qualities required in a bishop were: university studies (there were Salamanca professors, and numerous masters and doctors of theology), experience in administration (monastic priors, Franciscan Guardians, deans of ecclesiastical chapters, Presidents of the Inquisition, etc.), and almost always proven virtue and poverty. In this sense, the Council certainly chose in a way that could not have been bettered by either the churches of the *conquistadores* or Rome itself.[4]

Once a short list of candidates (from one to three) for a particular see had been drawn up, those chosen were given an "advice" in writing. They did not always accept the candidature, but if they did, their names were "presented" to the pope in Rome by the Spanish ambassador. The pope could delay the presentations, but very few were refused. The Roman Consistory debated the names at one meeting and gave its decision after taking a vote a few days later. The Cardinal Protector of Castile took the "responsibilities" before the Consistory, and the consistorial charters bore the date of the meeting at which the vote was taken. After prolonged procedures involving corrections, legalizations, confrontations, copies, etc., the Bull was registered at the Lateran chancellery, and charges were paid in the Apostolic Chamber.

Meanwhile, since these procedures were lengthy, the Council

---

[4] Cf. *Les évêques hispano-americains*, p. 49.

customarily gave those who had been elected and presented a Royal Charter of "request and command", armed with which they could leave for America without waiting for the Bull, pressent it to the civil and ecclesiastical authorities there and take preparatory charge of some of their pastoral functions. This custom was criticized by St Toribio, archbishop of Lima.

When the Council received the Bull of appointment of the bishop, it sent what were known as his "executive orders" (a Royal Charter allowing him to perform what he had been appointed by the pope to perform). Without these, the bishop could not take definite charge of his bishopric, nor was a council or synod or any other ecclesiastical event in the Indies recognized as valid.

As an example of the time scale of this procedure, Pablo de Talavera, bishop of Tlaxcala, was *elected* by the Council on 29 August 1543, *named* by the Consistory on 2 April 1544, and received his *executive orders* on 17 October the same year. He reached his diocese on 24 July 1548, was *consecrated* on 7 April 1549, and died on 19 October 1557.

For a bishop to receive his executive orders, it was usual to require from him an "oath of fidelity"[5] to the "patronage", after which he could be consecrated bishop—in America, with one bishop only officiating, and using native balsam.[6] But the patronage system required even more than this. To be able to take charge of his diocese, the new bishop had to present his executive orders and the Bull (or the Royal Charter of "request and command") to the Viceroy, Audience, Governor or secular Chapter at the same time as to the ecclesiastical Chapter that had been administering the diocese as a *sede vacante*. All this was a source of endless quarrels, since so many different authorities and patronal rights produced a continual stream of interferences, conflicts and contradictions.

Because of "patronage", the King possessed, through the Council of the Indies, a juridical system that allowed him to dominate the Church completely, though the Church, in its daily activities, was always trying to escape from this omnipotence. On the other hand, "patronage" effectively prevented Rome from exercising any influence whatsoever in America. *Propaganda fide* (established in 1623) was unable to obtain any foothold in Latin America till well into the nineteenth century. The Papal Nuncio in Madrid never succeeded in appointing a nuncio in America, although the King was not successful either in establishing a patriarchate there with genuinely autonomous ecclesiastical powers.

III. The Sociography of the Appointment of Bishops

To judge how the system actually worked, some figures will enable one to form a quantitative judgment.

Between 1511 and the end of 1620, 292 candidates were chosen and presented to Rome by the King and the Council. 243 presentations were named by consistorial Bull, involving 159 resident bishops (with 187 periods of ecclesiastical government). Fernando (d. 1516) did not present any Creole candidates, his successor Charles V (abdicated in 1555) presented only 3·1% Creoles, as did Philip II (d. 1598), whereas Philip III's choices were 38% Creole. Of these, 33% were secular clergy, 32% Dominican friars (who acted brilliantly in defence of the Indians), and the remainder Franciscans, Augustinians, etc. Of the twenty-three Creole bishops presented, twelve came from Mexico, four from Lima, and one each from Cusco, Arequipa and other places.

Of more concern in assessing the patronage system is the time that elapsed during the process of nominating a bishop. The average duration of the hundred and eighty-seven periods of government was twelve years nine months, but four years eight months of this was a period of *sede vacante*, so the bishop's effective average period of residence was eight years one month. A more significant picture emerges from a comparison by archbishoprics or regions (see table below).

This shows that there was actually one archdiocese—La Plata, comprising Chuquisaca and present-day Argentina, Bolivia and Paraguay—in which the total time of *sede vacante* was higher than that of effective occupation. At the time, the route between Spain and this region was via the Pacific coast of South America, so news of the death of a bishop had to travel back via Peru and the Panama-Caribbean region and across the North Atlantic. The new bishop then had to follow this route in reverse. From this point of view the patronage system was badly adapted to the immense distances involved. The situation was better in Santa Fe de Bogotá (present-day Colombia), whose percentage of vacant time was the lowest, even though Santo Domingo was better situated geographically.

Comparison of the total time in months of *sede vacante* and effective government by the resident bishop—1511–1620

Archdiocese or region	Months of residence by the bishop	Months of *sede vacante*	Percentage of time vacant
Santo Domingo	3,344	1,765	34·5
Central America	3,586	1,809	33·5
Mexico	3,733	1,485	28·4
Santa Fe	2,656	841	24·0
Lima	3,627	2,994	45·2
La Plata	1,250	1,459	53·8
Total	18,196	10,553	36·2

Cf. *Les évêques hispano-américains*, pp. 37–44.

Such comparative studies help to give a better idea of the workings of patronage, and enable one to evaluate its scope, advantages and limitations in the sixteenth century.

IV. "Patronage" of Colonial Christendom and its Crisis

In an earlier *Concilium* article,[7] I discussed the crisis in science produced by the transition from Christendom (understood as a "cultural" entity including Christianity) to a secular civilization in which Christianity recovered a healthy independence, enabling it better to face up to its real universal mission. In the same way the gradual disappearance of what I have called "Latin American *colonial* Christendom" is now allowing the Church in Latin America, where it understands the meaning of the process, to become actively involved in the historical liberation of the continent, looking beyond the Spanish-European cultural patterns that have dominated it in the past.

[7] Cf. "From Secularization to Secularism: Science from the Renaissance to the Enlightenment", in *Concilium*, Sept. 1969 (American ed., vol. 47).

In the sixteenth century, the Latin American episcopate showed some outstanding qualities, and if the patronage system is to be judged on the basis of the people it chose and the way they behaved, then one can only conclude that it is one of the most fruitful periods in the history of the "reformed" episcopate in the Catholic Church. But quite soon, in the seventeenth and eighteenth centuries, the system began to groan under the oppressive weight of an excessively regalist institutionalization, and the bishop became no more than a cog in the Spanish colonial bureaucratic machine. As a result of this, the bishops played virtually no part in the "Wars of Independence" (1809–25), and even opposed the revolutionary and patriotic leanings of the younger and Creole clergy. The crisis of the nineteenth century, and the reaction that set in later (with the ideal of a "new Christendom" in the 1930s), have finally given way to a new attitude. The declarations of the Peruvian bishops in August 1971, made as proposals for the Synod, for example, demonstrate not only the possibility but also the need felt by many Christians to engage in a socialist course (not that of Marxism, rejected as bureaucratic and anti-democratic).

The situation of Latin America, and of its episcopate, as heirs of the only "colonial Christendom" in the world (Byzantium and Latin Europe were not *colonies*, nor were the Arab world, Africa and Asia *Christendoms*), places its bishops in the situation of being the *only* ones who can go through the struggle for the liberation of a continent in a post-Christendom condition. This unique situation should show historians of the European Churches that the Church in Latin America cannot simply be tacked on as a final appendix to the "history of the missions" (as histories of the Church in France, Germany, etc., have done up till now), because we are dealing with a whole "Christendom" (one of three with Byzantium and Rome, though politically dependent). The *sui generis* position of the Latin-American Church can only be described by its members, and so far there is not much call for its scholars to take their place in the studies, seminaries, joint works of history of the *European* Church, in effect, which sometimes pass as the history of the *universal* Catholic Church.

Translated by Paul Burns

Bernard Plongeron

The Practice of Democracy in the Constitutional Church of France (1790–1801)

THE Church of France, the child of the Civil Constitution of the Clergy of 12 July 1790, is despised by historians, who usually regard it as no more than a schismatic interlude in the life of Catholicism. And yet, behind the political decisions, the Constitutional Church taught and developed, until the Concordat of 1801, a theology and internal organization which in the light of Vatican II is impressively and admirably modern.

To understand their significance, we must find out what this Church was really like, in contrast to the caricatures offered by its opponents. Instead of imagining a handful of Gallican-Jansenist tub-thumpers, brought together by Abbé Grégoire with the aim of overthrowing Rome by means of the wild claims of demagogues, it would be necessary to rediscover the plan which these republican bishops and parish priests, many of whom were first-class theologians and who demonstrated their priestly courage during the crisis of the Terror, had for the Church.

It is worth while to recall this theology of the people of God, which grounded an elective principle bringing into play the consensus of bishops, priests and laity, with no schismatic intention and in conformity with the Civil Constitution of the Clergy. Like Lamourette in 1791, the bishop of the Meuse in 1801 explained his position: both maintained a unity of faith, of the priesthood (without presbyterianism), and of genuine communion with Rome. Here I can only sketch the stages by which these principles were applied from 1790 to 1801.

I. Under the Protection of the State: 1790–1793

In order to govern the eighty-five dioceses established by the new regime, with their thousands of parishes, section II of the Civil Constitution of the Clergy laid down electoral procedure in detail, in departmental assemblies for the bishops and district assemblies for the priests. Two candidates were put forward. An absolute majority was requisite at the first vote, and a bare majority at the subsequent votes. The elder was elected if the votes were equal (cf. the Decree of 22 December 1789). Canonical requirements were laid down for the candidates: ten years of service in a parish for candidates for bishop, and five for candidates for parish priest. Canonical investiture was in the hands of the metropolitan, who could not refuse it except "after having consulted with the whole clergy of his church" (art. XVI). The bishop had to discuss with his council the institution of parish priests, whose election "will be carried out by separate votes for each vacant parish" (art. XXVIII). "In no case will there be any appeal except from the bishop to the diocesan synod and from the metropolitan to the metropolitan synod" (section I, art. V). Every active citizen who was an elector to the civil assembly could take part in the church elections. The bishop's council had a consultative function and consisted of members selected by a double procedure: episcopal vicars chosen by the diocesan, and superiors of religious houses and directors of the seminary, who themselves were *elected in synod* "by means of separate ballots and with an absolute majority of votes". They could not be deprived except in a synod, on a complaint laid by the bishop with knowledge of the facts (section II, art. XXIV). The legislator obviously intended to guarantee the independence of the elected member, within the council, against episcopal vicars who might be the "creatures" of the bishop and no longer have opinions of their own. This was a wise precaution, for in many dioceses experience was to show the servility of the episcopal vicars, whose suppression was called for in 1793. Although the parish priest chose his curates in the same way as the bishop his vicars, he had direct power over them. The curate had hardly any legal recourse against his parish priest.

In practice, and although the bishop of 1791 had much in

common with his predecessor under the Ancien Régime as far as personal and effective power was concerned, the procedure suffered from the complications and exceptions inherent in the political situation in the diocese. At the episcopal level, the civil authorities thought nothing of putting pressure on the electors. Thus the authorities of the *Société des Amis la Révolution et de la Liberté* at Soissons conducted an electoral campaign, in January 1791, on behalf of Abbé Grégoire, "parish priest of Emberminil (*sic*)" for his election to the see of the Aisne. Lafont de Savine, consecrated bishop of Viviers in 1778, one of the five bishops of the Ancien Régime to accept the Civil Constitution of the Clergy, made a great show of submitting to the laws of democracy. He resigned in order to be reinstated by popular vote. Going beyond the provisions of the Constitution, he made his episcopal vicars stand for election by the parish priests during a sumptuous banquet given in the park of his episcopal residence. In some places we hear of numerous Protestants and even Jews (in Alsace and Gard) as well as women in the electoral assemblies. But in general the procedure at episcopal elections followed the rules, the minutes were scrupulously kept, and the ceremonial of investiture observed perfectly.

The main sources of difficulty lay elsewhere. Presentation to parishes depended upon the geographical spread of priests who had taken the oath, and the rate of retractations. On various pretexts, those elected did not all accept the post to which they were sent. "In Sarthe, a quarter refused, in Ardèche, in Maine-et-Loire and the Vendée, three-quarters or at least a half."[1]

The result was that the system laid down by the Constituent Assembly was increasingly flouted. The length of service necessary to be nominated parish priest was reduced; priests from one department were allowed to stand in another; religious were drawn upon; and worse still, the bishops were given authority to nominate priests-in-charge.

Irregularities of this sort did not prevent the concerted action resulting from a church government that was both hierarchical and collegial from leading to methodical and fruitful work. In

[1] J. Leflon, *La crise révolutionnaire 1789-1846*, Vol. 20 of *L'Histoire de l'Église* (Paris, 1949), p. 76.

1791, the thirteen episcopal vicars of the council of Loir-et-Cher, under the direction of Grégoire, shared out their tasks not on the pattern of the former archdeaconries, but on that of the districts. When parish priests addressed their request to the bishop they were to mark them "ecclesiastical affairs", so that every member of the council could know of them. This was a neat way of indicating that there is no longer any sphere reserved to the bishop. Did this mean that the episcopal council was comparable to the Supreme Soviet? This is not so, and the State took care that episcopal prerogatives were respected. A notable example is where the bishop, as a member of the National Assembly, could no longer ensure the regular fulfilment of his functions in his diocese. As at Blois in the case of Grégoire, an order of the Departmental Directory of 25 May 1792 confers upon the chief vicar, Servier, for the church of Lyons, "the acts of jurisdiction which do not require the episcopal character". These acts could only be carried out on the "advice of the council", according to article XLI of the law of 24 August 1790.

Whether or not the Church remained master of the situation depended upon the interplay of personalities and influences within the council. Diverse reactions towards the marriage of priests from 1792 onwards are characteristic in this respect. At Paris, four parish priests combined in 1793 to denounce the scandalous decision of the council of Bishop Gobel to institute, as the new parish priest of Saint-Augustin, Aubert, a curate who married in 1792. "Surely the bishop cannot claim to be in charge of discipline throughout his diocese to such an extent that he thinks his personal authority, *without even consulting his presbyterate, and of which we form an essential part,* entitles him to do away with all general and particular, apostolic and modern regulations, without cause, without necessity, and for no good and plausible reason...?"[2] On the other hand, in March 1793, the episcopal council of Nord debated whether a married man who wished to remain in the married state could be admitted to orders. At the first session, the voting was equal. The bishop did not wish to give a casting vote. At a second meeting, on 29 March, the coun-

[2] *Réclamation adressée aux Evêques de France par des curés de Paris ...* (Paris, June 1793).

cil voted in favour after hearing a long memorandum prepared by the second vicar.[3] Co-operation could easily turn into sometimes violent dispute, as the difficulties of the year 1793 grew greater. The bishop of the Somme, Desbois de Rochefort, one of the most outstanding personalities of the constitutional clergy, decided to rid himself of some of his episcopal vicars whom he regarded as too turbulent. The pretext he used was the decree of 1 July 1793 requiring bishops to send their surplus vicars to be priests-in-charge of the disendowed parishes in their diocese. The two vicars he had in mind joined with their colleagues in the council to protest to the civil authorities. The chief vicar, Brandicourt, pointed to his twenty-three years in charge of one of the most important parishes in Amiens, and recalled that he had forced the bishop to a further ballot at the two first votes in the episcopal election. On 12 August, the two elected commissioners, Peyssard and Lacost, rejected the bishop's decision on the ground that he was exceeding his powers.

This was one of the last interventions of the State in the internal government of the Church. Soon afterwards the State did not recognize the privileged status of the Church.

II. BETWEEN THE CHARGE OF FEUDALISM AND ANARCHY (1793-1795)

"A privileged status"—a fatal charge for an individual or a body in 1793—was the somewhat paradoxical accusation made against the national Church. According to P. C. F. Bert,[4] its organization, based upon the civil institution, was democratic in appearance only. In his view, this is a result of the persistence of traditional offices, which always made churchmen "an order, and *the first order in the State*. This order has an existence so separate and independent of the authorities that in it not bodies but individuals form the legal hierarchy that constitutes it. One priest is a metropolitan, a bishop, etc. . . . By contrast, the departments, districts, municipalities and tribunals exist only because they are composed of a certain quantity of citizens, and because these in-

[3] *La Feuille Villageoise*, 42, 19 July 1792, pp. 369–70.
[4] *Des prêtres salariés par la nation considérés dans leurs rapports avec le gouvernement républicain* (Paris, 1793).

dividuals are gathered together where their meetings are taking place: none of their members is anything outside this meeting place, and none has any authority on his own..." (p. 21). Somewhat illogically, the same writer protests further on against the form of independence which the Constituent Assembly had created for parish priests: "The parish priest has nothing to fear from the council, which never hears anything of him, and never tries in any way to find out how he behaves" (p. 69). There is no mutual emulation, because the parish priest has nothing to look forward to after he is elected; he need not fear being called to order by a bishop trying to keep the goodwill of his council and consequently avoiding delicate inquiries, by contrast to the chief vicar of the past, to whom this Republican writer looks back with some nostalgia. This tendentious work drew attention to a gap in the new system: the absence of pastoral visitations, which in certain dioceses the parish priests refused as a survival of despotism. In 1797, the bishop of Amiens complained of the discredit into which the episcopal function had fallen: "The most sacred rules of ecclesiastical discipline have been broken: one might say that the church is without government. The parishes think that they can enjoy the benefits of Catholic worship and do without the parish priests; and if the bishop were not absolutely necessary for ordination and confirmation, his ministry would be called upon by no more than a tiny number of priests; he would not even be able to exercise his authority without danger to himself."[5] The bishop of the Jura, Moise, described the disarray and confusion created in the parishes during the year II. In one place the Terror led to the desertion of a parish, in another it installed, in breach of an interdict, priests who had renounced their orders, had married or were simply in rebellion. He affirmed that ninety-eight per cent of his parish priests alleged to be in office in 1795 no longer possessed the legal document recording their election "and those who did have it, what did they possess? Improper and fundamentally invalid documents." He also attacked the institution of episcopal vicars, "new canons", seizing all powers for themselves and often unworthy in their conduct. "Unfortu-

[5] *Lettre pastorale de l'évêque d'Amiens pour la convocation du Synode diocéain* ... (Paris, May 1797).

nately it was not thought possible in 1790, after the enlargement of the dioceses and the division of parishes, that all the parish priests, as co-operators with the bishop, could form his presbyterate and could be members of his council."[6]

These reflections, with others, interpreted the experience of those who survived the persecution and permitted them to make use of the freedom of worship decreed by the Convention in 1795 to plan a total reshaping of the national Church, now set free from the Civil Constitution of the Clergy.

III. A NEW CHURCH ORGANIZATION (1795–1801)

The moment the churches were reopened, in the spring of 1795, a committee of "United Bishops" (*Évêques réunis*) was formed at Paris under the leadership of Grégoire, bishop of Loir-et-Cher, with the assistance of the metropolitan bishop of Rouen, the bishops of the Somme, the Landes and the Ain. Three of them, Grégoire (Blois), Saurine (Dax) and Royer (Bellay) were former members of the Convention. In order to reach dioceses throughout the country, to publicize their decisions, and to get the pastoral and doctrinal movement under way again, they founded the *Annales de la Religion*, of which Grégoire and Desbois were joint editors. On 15 March 1795, by way of their periodical, the United Bishops sent an *"Encyclical Letter to their Brothers, the Other Bishops, and to the Churches without Bishops"*, which was also a manifesto of the religious revival, a profession of Roman Catholic faith, a charter for the reorganization of the Church which resulted from the reaction of Thermidor (27 July 1794), and an appeal for a national council.

Under the heading of reorganization, they specified as an urgent requirement that the bishop was to have two councils: the first was a survival of that set up by the Civil Constitution of the Clergy, the opinion of which must be taken regarding every general regulation to be applied in the diocese. The second was a creation inspired by the *presbyterium* of apostolic times, which included *all* priests regularly employed by the bishop. It must

---

[6] *Procès-verbal d'actes du Synode diocésain de Saint-Claude* (5–6 August 1800), unbound, no date.

have twelve members at least, and in ordinary administration the bishop "will do nothing important without having conferred with them". Another innovation is that if the see is vacant, the government of the diocese is taken over by the presbytery.

From the very first, the new organization was distinguished from that of 1790 by a collegiality of the bishops as a body, and of the priests with their bishop, together with a number of laymen who had the right to speak. Thirty bishops and three metropolitan presbyteries (Paris, Lyons and Angers) followed the *Encyclical Letter* and set about organizing diocesan presbyteries where they did not yet exist. The authority of the bishop was not yet clearly defined, as was admitted by one of the United Bishops, Gratian, metropolitan of Rouen. In 1797, he wrote to Grégoire: "It is certain that the bishop is obliged to consult the clergy of his own diocese on important matters; but a question which it seems to me remains undecided is whether he is obliged to follow the majority of even the virtual unanimity of pastors of the second rank. I see clearly that he cannot make a decision against their unanimous view. In any case he would do so in vain. But I do not see so clearly that he may not abstain from a decision in this case."[7] Nevertheless, the central and painful issue remained the election of new bishops following the death, retirement or abdication during the Terror of those who held the post in 1791. In 1795, more than a quarter of the dioceses of 1790 were "widowed churches". What electoral procedure was to be followed? What control could there be when the State no longer offered its official guarantee?

In one of the most important decrees, *On Elections* (eight sections) the National Council of August–November 1797, at which there were a hundred and one participants (thirty-one bishops and seventy priest delegates, with six theologians as experts) set about adapting the former Civil Constitution of the Clergy to the experience of the Church after 1795, and to the recasting of territorial divisions in the Constitution of the year III (1795).

Apostolic authority was handed down by *election* and *ordination*, to use Bossuet's expression, from pastor to pastor, from bishop to bishop. There was an absolute respect for electoral free-

---

[7] *Bibl. Soc. de Port-Royal*, Grégoire correspondance, Seine Inférieure file.

dom: "It is of little importance whether the people and the clergy take part in the election together or whether one or other of them takes the initiative." The procedure of acclamation may even be used. But in order to be an elector, one must be a Catholic and twenty-one years of age, which the former Constitution did not lay down. More attention was paid than ever before to canonical institution, preceded in certain cases by a virtual interrogation on the subject of morals and faith, and also upon the past conduct of the candidate for consecration.[8] If for any reason the election of the bishop was not completed within two months, the metropolitan acting with his suffragans had an unrestricted right to nominate him. This was done in the case of Aubert, metropolitan of the Côtes de la Mediterranée, nominated in 1798 by his three suffragans of the Var, the Basses-Alpes and the Vaucluse, but acclaimed on the day of his consecration by the presbytery of Aix. There is a new intermediate authority: the archpriest, "The eye of the bishop", elected by a synod based on the *arrondissement* and living in the *canton* (the sub-division of a department). The election of a parish priest was to be made from a list of three candidates, presented by the archpriest to the bishop: the laity were to vote on this list. In every election a majority of two-thirds of the votes was required. The curates continued to be chosen by the parish priest, but with the consent of the bishop; and they could not be removed except for good reason.

The real innovation lay in the activity of the diocesan synods, which were real diocesan parliaments in matters of doctrine and discipline, in which the laity could take part. The meetings of these synods were slow in getting under way, but were in full swing in 1800 for the preparation of the second National Council, in which priests of the second rank were more important as delegates than in 1797. By then thirty-five dioceses had held their first synod (the model of which remains that of the Jura with 168 participants). Between 1789 and 1800 fifty-three dioceses called their synod together for the first time.

Thus the twenty-five thousand or so members of the Constitu-

---

[8] *Questions faites au R. Évêque élu de Versailles par son Métropolitan et Réponses* (Paris, 1797).

tional Church, on the eve of the Concordat, were subject to a discipline which was not without its weaknesses, either in the form of internal struggles (e.g., the battle over the metropolitan of Paris) or of the ill-will and open opposition of the civil authorities; but at every level in the hierarchy they had recovered a sense of collegiality never before achieved in the Church in France. There was a reminder of this after the Revolution of 1830, when certain churchmen demanded a return to the elective and collegial principle.[9]

Translated by R. A. Wilson

---

[9] *Du système électif étendu aux membres du clergé ou de la promotion aux évêchés et aux curés* (Paris, September 1832).

Robert Trisco

Democratic Influence on the Election of Bishops and Pastors and on the Administration of Dioceses and Parishes in the U.S.A.

AMERICAN Catholics, whether natives or immigrants, have almost universally admired their country's democratic form of government, and some of them have even tried to incorporate it as far as possible into their ecclesiastical polity. Though they have sometimes been unconscious of the influence of their milieu, they have deliberately made such attempt for one or more of several reasons: defensive (to forestall attacks deriving from suspicion of the Church's hierarchical structure and thus to preserve the religious freedom of a beleaguered minority); apologetical (to lessen the American Church's subjection to foreign control, which was an obstacle to the conversion of their fellow citizens); and reformist (to strengthen the Church internally by adopting procedures that had already been proved beneficial in the political sphere).

The clergy's desire to use a democratic procedure in the choosing of their bishops was manifested very early in the history of the republic.[1] When John Carroll was appointed first superior of the whole American mission by the Congregation de Propaganda Fide in 1784, he was informed that the pope intended soon to name a vicar apostolic, who would be a titular bishop. Carroll replied that a residential bishop, who would be less dependent on the Roman congregation, was much to be preferred and that a bad feeling might be excited among the people of the

[1] Peter Guilday, *The Life and Times of John Carroll, Archbishop of Baltimore (1735–1815)* (Westminster, Maryland, 1954; reprint of 1922), pp. 203, 220–2, 348, 569.

country, both Catholic and Protestant, if the priests were not allowed to propose a candidate to the Holy See. In 1788 the clergy requested that an episcopal see be erected, that those who were duly exercising the religious ministry and had the care of souls be permitted to elect the bishop, and that thereafter elections be regularly conducted, in order that the false opinions regarding the Catholic religion which had imbued the minds of Protestants might be completely refuted. Besides these stated motives, they made these requests also because they wished to ensure the choice of one of their own number of ex-Jesuits before other priests coming from Europe would attain a majority. Upon the Propaganda's recommendation, Pius VI authorized them to select the see city and to elect the first occupant. After they had agreed on Baltimore and voted almost unanimously for Carroll, the pope ratified their decisions, issuing the bull in 1789.

The fear that the American government or a large number of American Protestants might object to the direct appointment of bishops by the Holy See remained sufficiently alive to win for Carroll permission to consult his clergy before proposing a priest as his coadjutor. He was told by the Propaganda, however, that the privilege of election, which had been granted to the clergy for one time only, could not be allowed again even though a direct appointment by Rome might be interpreted by enemies of the Church in the republic as violating the spirit of the Constitution. Carroll conducted the consultation of the clergy, nevertheless, in the form of an election. When the man elected, Lawrence Graessl, died before he could be consecrated, Carroll, upon the advice of the older members of the clergy, nominated another ex-Jesuit, Leonard Neale, who was then officially appointed by the pope. Thereafter no formal participation in the choice of candidates for the episcopate was vouchsafed to priests until the Third Plenary Council of Baltimore in 1884. Not only did the Propaganda wish to keep a close watch over the nascent church, but the bishops themselves were not disposed to share their right of recommendation with the many priests who had not yet proved their trustworthiness by long and faithful service in the diocese.

Having seen the priests elect their first bishop, the laity in some places wished to elect their own pastors. Their effort to

introduce a democratic element on the parochial level was facilitated by the system of lay trustees required by civil law in most
of the states. Although the abuse of this institution, generally
called "trusteeism", had European roots, it sprang partly from
an express desire to make the Catholic parish resemble the con-
gregational form of organization prevalent among American
Protestants. Strangely enough, it was two groups of German
Catholics, one in Philadelphia and the other in Baltimore, who
were among the first to invoke American laws in support of their
demands.[2] In each case the Germans separated themselves from
the existing territorial mission, elected trustees, built a church,
and appointed a pastor—all in defiance of Carroll's authority.
In Philadelphia one of the successive pastors was also dismissed
by the trustees, who wrote to the Holy See in 1799 with great
exaggeration that they had received from the legislature of the
State of Pennsylvania the right to make any ordinances which
would not be contrary to the divine or civil laws. In Baltimore
too the trustees, appealing to Rome against Bishop Carroll, asserted that the United States gave unrestricted liberty to every
nationality of every religious persuasion and prohibited that anyone should be disturbed by another in this liberty or should
violate it. These Germans, of course, did not base their claims
solely or even principally upon American laws; rather they de-
fended their right to elect their pastor on virtue of the *ius patronatus*. Even if, nevertheless, they invoked those laws only as
weapons in their struggle against Carroll, they obviously were
contending that their mode of naming pastors was more in keeping with the national spirit than appointment by the bishop.

Although both these German parishes eventually abandoned
their pretensions, refractory trustees in other cities provoked more
serious troubles after Carroll's death. Those in Norfolk, Virginia,
sustained by most of the Irish parishioners and led by a clever
Portuguese physician, Dr John F. Oliveira Fernandez, rejected
the French pastor whom Archbishop Neale had sent to them
and asserted their right to administer their church indepen-

[2] V. J. Fecher, s.v.d., *A Study of the Movement for German National
Parishes in Philadelphia and Baltimore (1787–1802)* (Analecta Gregoriana,
77; Rome, 1955), *passim*, esp. pp. 255-6.

dently.[3] Soon these schismatics made common cause with the rebellious trustees of Charleston, South Carolina, and in a lengthy "Petition to the Holy See" upheld their assumed right of patronage and presented to the pope an Irish Dominican in New York, Thomas Carbry, for confirmation as first bishop of Norfolk. After further dissension Carbry reported to the Italian prior· of the Dominican convent of the Minerva in Rome that if a priest could be found who would consent to be consecrated by the Jansenist archbishop of Utrecht, he would be heartily welcomed in the United States. Carbry predicted that petitions would be presented to Congress and to the legislatures of the different states that no ecclesiastic of whatever grade "be permitted to exercise any function in the Republic, unless elected by the people". His prediction was verified in December 1818, when an anonymous open letter, printed as a broadside, was sent to many American statesmen, maintaining that the appointment of bishops by the pope was a temporal act, and praising the elective system as "perfectly conforming to the fundamental and vital principles of the American constitution", as well as just and reasonable in itself and common for nearly a thousand years in the Church. Although the Irish Franciscan who had been chosen by the leaders of the Charleston schism to found an "Independent Catholic Church" in the United States denounced the scheme to the Propaganda, Carbry accepted the pastorate of the Norfolk church to which the trustees had elected him. It was mainly out of fear of a permanent schism that the Propaganda decided hastily to found episcopal sees in Richmond, Virginia, and in Charleston and to fill them with priests from Ireland.

To prevent a recurrence of the evils which had arisen out of the maladministration of church property, the first bishop of Charleston, John England, having studied the church order of several Protestant denominations and the character of the government and the people of the country as well as the circumstances of his diocese, drew up an elaborate constitution.[4] The bishop

[3] Peter Guilday, *The Catholic Church in Virginia (1815-1822)* (United States Catholic Historical Society Monograph Series, VIII; New York, 1924), *passim*, esp. pp. 33, 46, 81, 91-101 and 105.
[4] Peter Guilday, *The Life and Times of John England, First Bishop of Charleston (1786-1842)* (New York, 1927), I, 349-51, 362-3.

alone was to have the right to appoint or remove clergymen, but each of the three districts of the diocese was to have a vestry, consisting of the clergymen and a number of elected laymen, for the management of the temporalities; there was also to be a general fund administered by a board of trustees of which the bishop was *ex officio* president. Each year a convention was to be held, made up of three parts—the bishop, the House of the Clergy and the House of the Lay Delegates; the role of these houses was mainly to advise the bishop, to raise funds and to superintend the persons who had charge of the money. England's metropolitan, Ambrose Maréchal of Baltimore, though he had not seen it, warned the Propaganda against approving this "democratic constitution", because he feared that other bishops would not be able to keep the clergy and laity under control. Actually, England had not submitted the constitution to Rome, nor did the Propaganda ever sanction or censure it. It was not adopted by any of England's episcopal colleagues, however, and it was buried with him in 1842. Everywhere else too by 1860 the bishops overcame the threat of trusteeism by depriving the laity of any effective voice in the management of even the purely temporal affairs of their own parishes.

At the same time, the priests had no share in the administration of their diocese, since there were no cathedral chapters of canons and even where consultors existed they could not limit the bishop's authority.[5] In 1857 the Archbishop of St Louis, Peter Richard Kenrick, recommended to the Holy See the erection of cathedral chapters in the United States, because, in his opinion, it would help to remove the suspicion and odium that the bishops incurred, especially among non-Catholics, by managing temporal affairs alone and without any check on their power. Most of the American bishops, however, voted against his proposal in the Second Plenary Council of Baltimore in 1866, and in the Third they yielded to the insistence of the Propaganda only after substituting consultors for canons and after eliminating the proposed requirement of the consultors' consent for the legality of

[5] Robert Trisco, "Bishops and Their Priests in the United States", in *The Catholic Priest in the United States: Historical Investigations*, ed. John Tracy Ellis (Collegeville, Minnesota, 1971), pp. 111–292, esp. 138–49, 228–31 and 238–9.

certain episcopal actions. On behalf of his colleagues, the Archbishop of Baltimore, James Gibbons, had protested to the Propaganda that chapters did not accord with the character of the American people, apparently implying that his democratic compatriots were not in favour of shared responsibility and accountability. According to the conciliar decree, the bishop was to choose half of the consultors freely and the other half from a list proposed by the diocesan clergy, but this restriction, which seldom hindered a bishop in practice from appointing only those who would defer to his will, was abolished by the Code of Canon Law.

The same plenary council conferred on priests an enlarged role in the selection of candidates for the episcopate.[6] Occasionally, in the preceding decades, certain priests had publicly expressed their dissatisfaction at being completely excluded from the procedure, but it was only on the eve of the council that Patrick Corrigan, pastor of the Church of Our Lady of Hope in Hoboken, New Jersey, in a pamphlet entitled "Episcopal Nominations" argued that "a certain qualified number" of priests "should have the power of nominating the bishops". The alleged occasion for his writing was a European tour during which he had observed "the deplorable state of religion in Italy, France and Spain" which he attributed to the reluctance of certain conservative prelates in those co-called Catholic countries to tolerate a greater measure of political democracy, and he wished to forewarn his fellow American Catholics lest the Church in the United States also lose its influence over the masses. He saw no apparent reason for ignoring, in the mode of naming bishops, "the fundamental doctrine of the land—the principle of self-government". In another pamphlet he denied that he was trying to introduce revolutionary principles into the Church, or to Americanize it "by advancing democratic demands on the part of priests hitherto unheard of" that would tend to destroy it; he insisted, nevertheless, that the Church should anticipate the wish of the American people by conforming its laws to the instincts of the country whenever possible—particularly in regard to representation and the preven-

[6] Robert Trisco, "The Variety of Procedures in Modern History", in *The Choosing of Bishops*, ed. William W. Bassett (Hartford, Connecticut, 1971), pp. 33–60, esp. 51–9, and more extensively in the article cited above in footnote 5.

tion of "the arbitrary exercise of absolute power". By this time (May 1884) Corrigan looked to the forthcoming council for the fulfilment of his desires. The council did, indeed—but only under pressure from the Propaganda—decree that some priests in each diocese (namely, the consultors and irremovable rectors) should be allowed to present a terna. In spite of local difficulties caused by rivalries among groups of different foreign origins and by violations of secrecy, this method remained in effect until 1916, when it was replaced by a new one in which no collective consultation of the clergy was permitted and individual consultation in secrecy was left to the discretion of the bishops.

Those who attempted to introduce democratic ideals and practices into the Church maintained that their proposed reforms were consonant with genuine Catholic tradition. For the most part they seem to have sincerely believed that by these changes they would not merely conform to the values and mores of their society, but could make church structures less alien to Protestants and more advantageous to Catholics themselves. In their enthusiasm or obstinacy, some of them gave scandal rather than edification to non-Catholics and promoted discord rather than progress within the Church. Far from discrediting their goals, such mistakes provide useful lessons for the present, and many of their theoretical arguments and practical achievements furnish positive precedents for certain reforms being advocated today.

PART II
BULLETIN

Owen Chadwick

The Anglican Practice in the Election of Bishops

IN THE later Middle Ages English kings acquired, with the com‑
plaisance of the popes, the substantial part in the nomination of
bishops for election by the chapters to English sees. During the
fifteenth century this part of the king increased. The English
Reformation abolished the interventions of the pope and made
fully legal the sole rights of the king to nominate bishops for
election. The Annates Act of 1534, which is still (1972) partly
in force in England, provided that at every vacancy the king
may grant a licence to the dean and chapter of the cathedral to
proceed to an election (the *congé d'élire*) with a letter containing
the name of the person whom they shall choose. If the dean and
chapter shall delay for more than twelve days after they receive
the licence, the king may appoint a man to be bishop by letters
patent. If the dean and chapter delay to elect for more than
twenty days (and if the archbishop refuse to confirm the king's
candidate within twenty days) then the dean and chapter, or the
archbishop, are liable to the penalties laid down by the medieval
acts of *Praemunire* (especially the statute of Praemunire 1393);
those penalties being to place the convicted person outside the
Crown's protection and render him liable to the confiscation of
his lands and goods.

The sovereigns after the Reformation were not so well‑in‑
formed about church affairs that they did not need advice in
making their choice of bishops. Sometimes that adviser was a
lay minister, as Sir William Cecil (Lord Burghley) advised Queen
Elizabeth I (1558–98). Sometimes it was an ecclesiastic, as William

Laud advised King Charles I (1625–41). Twice, after the restoration of King Charles II in 1660 and again after the "revolution" in 1688, it was normally a commission—the Archbishop of Canterbury, the Bishop of London, and four laymen—but the advice of the Commissioners was often ignored by the Crown and its chief minister. When King George I came to the throne in 1714 he could not speak English, and was very ignorant about the Church of England. The Prime Minister quickly became a dominant force in government, and it was soon established that the king did not nominate bishops except on his advice. Henceforth the king (or queen) suggested names, and frequently disapproved of names suggested. But the initiating power in nomination lay with the prime minister. The king or queen had only a veto, and even before Queen Victoria the veto became possible only where the prime minister felt sufficiently indifferent not to threaten to resign if he did not get his way. That was still often, and Queen Victoria (1837–1901), especially in her latter years, exercised an informed influence upon the appointments. The Archbishop of Canterbury was throughout consulted as a matter of courtesy, and where the queen took a part he could be very influential. It should be noticed that Parliament has never had any share in the choice of bishops; except in so far as its support is necessary to the position of a prime minister.

After Queen Victoria's death in 1901 three things made a difference: (a) King Edward VII (1901–10) knew much less about it than his mother, and cared less, (b) the first non-Anglican prime minister was Arthur Balfour (prime minister 1901–05), which caused scruples to some Anglicans about the part played by the prime minister, and (c) the movement towards autonomy of the Church of England, partly descended from the Oxford Movement, had grown so far as to create (1904) a representative organ, or "synod", of the Church, in the so-called "Representative Church Council" (later, 1919, called Church Assembly, and since 1970 called General Synod). After 1901 there was more criticism of the prime minister's part, and more desire by church bodies to exercise influence in the choice of bishops; and the sovereign himself (or herself) interfered much less frequently.

The Crown's right to nominate has been called in question on occasions when a particularly controversial appointment has been made. In 1918 the Crown (prime minister, Lloyd George) nominated to the see of Hereford, Hensley Henson, who was believed not to accept the historicity of the great miracles of the New Testament. The Convocation of Canterbury appointed a committee (chairman, Bishop Winnington-Ingram of London) to consider how the Church could play a greater part in the choice of bishops. The only thing which came out of this committee was a request that the prime minister might always consult the Archbishops of Canterbury and York before nominating. Lloyd George replied that he always did so. It appears that at least from this date the Archbishop of York, like the Archbishop of Canterbury, has been consulted as a matter of courtesy. At the present time (1972) the prime minister chooses one name from four or five names all of whom have been privately "approved" as suitable by the two archbishops.

A second committee of Church Assembly in 1923 recommended that the dean and chapter should not be liable to the penalties of Praemunire if they refused to accept the Crown's nomination. This was not given effect till 1969, when Praemunire was quietly abolished. The medieval statute had of course long been impossible to enforce.

The same committee of 1923 recommended that before the prime minister advised the Crown he should himself be advised by a commission of the two archbishops and five others chosen by the prime minister from the Church Assembly. Nothing was done about this. The archbishops themselves have tended to feel that the safeguards for the Church in the modern system were ample, and have had no special desire to be surrounded by a committee in the advice which they give the prime minister. A 1935 Church and State Commission repudiated this 1923 proposal and rejected it. But members of the Church Assembly, and now of the General Synod, have felt that they, as the representative organ of the Church, ought to exercise some influence on the choice of persons advising the Crown; if indeed they ought not to provide for an electoral body itself. The Church and State Commission which reported in 1970 recommended that the Crown be advised by a committee chosen by General Synod. But the 1970 recommendation was hedged about by so much disagreement and so many qualifications that it is not likely to have much effect, not at least quickly.

Meanwhile the dioceses, as they became more organized and self-conscious through their diocesan conferences, began to wish to exert more influence upon the kind of man whom they were to receive as their new bishop. In 1939, Church Assembly agreed that at a vacancy representatives of the diocese should (without mentioning names) inform the archbishop of the needs of the diocese. At almost the same time—in the last year or so when Neville Chamberlain (who was a Unitarian) was prime minister, the prime minister began regularly, through one of his secretaries, to consult opinion in the diocese upon the kind of man (though not the name of the man) whom they wanted. In 1964 the Howick Commission on Crown Appointments recommended the creation of standing committees in each diocese, called Vacancy-in-See committees, to advise the prime minister and archbishop on the needs of the diocese with regard to the new bishop. These committees were created. And since 1966 they have begun to exert an important influence on the choice of men. In origin they were not supposed to express any opinion about individuals, but only about general needs. In fact they have increasingly refused to be deterred from mentioning the names of men whom they would like.

The present system works well. Good bishops get chosen. Yet it appears to be an interim system. It does not look like a system which can exist for very long, in precisely this form.

Many Anglicans in England (probably a considerable majority) like what happens. They like (on the whole) the bishops they get. They like their leaders to have a national, as well as an ecclesiastical, status. They like their bishops (the senior twenty-six) to sit in the House of Lords. They like them to be elected on the nomination of the queen, who must herself be a member of the Church of England. They see a system which works, and which has grown out of English history. They do not want to change it. Even some who do not much like it—even some who dislike the part of the prime minister very much—still value the national recognition of religion symbolized by the queen's nomination, and are prepared to endure the prime minister as an undesirable but necessary and innocuous accompaniment. They shrink from all the problems, and especially the possible measure of disendowment, attached to a national act of disestablishment.

Some Anglicans regard it quite differently—as the most offensive aspect of the relations between Church and State in England. Some of them want disestablishment. But some who do not want disestablishment for itself, prefer it to allowing the continuance of the prime minister's part. In the 1970 report of the Church and State Commission, exactly half the members recommended that the part of the prime minister should cease. Nevertheless five of that half of the commission recommended that the part of the queen should continue. But this is impossible. And here is the dilemma. Not to have the queen probably means a radical severance of Church and State. Yet you cannot have the queen without the prime minister.

Opinion on this matter changed even during the sixties.

In the 1964 Howick Report on Crown Appointments the members, though drawn from widely different schools of thought, were unanimous in recommending that nomination by the prime minister should continue.

In the report of the 1970 Church and State Commission, the members could reach no agreed conclusions.

Half of them argued: (a) our view of systems where bishops are elected does not lead us to like what happens; (b) it is unchristian, and bad theology, to distinguish sharply between a "secular" state and a "spiritual" Church; (c) bishops are more than diocesan pastors, they are national leaders; (d) to risk the disruption consequent on some national act of disestablishment is right if it is necessary—but those who want bishops elected are risking it to remedy no practical evil (since all agree that we get good bishops) and on purely doctrinaire grounds; (e) the checks on the prime minister's action are a sufficient safeguard for the Church's interests.

The other half argued: (a) in the modern secular world the choice of a secular authority is so obviously inappropriate that its inappropriateness does not need arguing; (b) the system is a historical survival, now passing out of context which made it meaningful; (c) the system has demerits—it all depends on men behaving well, there is little safeguard against them behaving ill; (d) free churchmen and Roman Catholics, with whom we wish to unite one day, are unanimous in disliking the system. They therefore proposed a choice by electoral board.

The existing situation carries within itself the seeds of change.

(*a*) It only requires a refusal by a dean and chapter to elect a person nominated—and no penalties now attach to that refusal—to precipitate a crisis. That is in effect the situation which has existed for more than a century, and no crisis has occurred. But the difference is that the diocese is now expressing its opinion beforehand—about needs, but increasingly about persons. The diocese has become conscious, not only of its interest, but of its power to influence the course of events, as never before. That consciousness is bound to grow further. The system works so long as the Crown works it with tender respect for the diocese's wishes and for the archbishops' wishes. It would hardly work if that respect ceased to exist.

(*b*) The personal intervention, both of the sovereign since 1901, and of the prime minister since 1939, has been less marked. The personal intervention of the prime minister is still important, but only between four or five carefully selected men. In the process of selecting those men the prime minister's secretary has played a part, but always in the closest consultation with the authorities of the Church both in the diocese and in the province. Therefore some argue that as the prime minister's part has tended to diminish, it will slowly become more and more formal.

There is a precedent for this development, in the case of suffragan bishops. By a statute of King Henry VIII, the diocesan bishop nominates two names to the king, who chooses one. Nowadays the diocesan bishop puts forward two names in his order of preference, and the Crown chooses by convention the first name. Even in the later Victorian age the ability of the Crown to choose between two names was not a formality. Gladstone once shocked the bishop of London by choosing the second name instead of the first. But with this exception, and one other possible exception, the Crown has chosen the first of the two names. And in modern times it has been argued to a prime minister that long custom now makes it impossible for him to choose any name but the first name.

As a matter of practice this is not a very good method of choosing suffragan bishops, because in effect it gives the sole right of choice to the diocesan bishop. Two different Commissions (Howick 1964, Chadwick 1970) have sought, so far vainly, to alter the system. But it shows how in a constitutional development the part of the prime minister may gradually and increasingly become a formality. In the judgment of some, this is one possibility with diocesan bishops. On the other hand, so long as election to a diocesan bishopric carries with it (sooner or later) automatic right to a seat in the House of Lords and therefore to a vote in Parliament, it is hard to conceive that the prime minister would allow his nomination to become a pure act of ritual—even though in recent times he has no longer concerned himself with the politics of the candidates. He became a mere formality in the choosing of suffragan bishops partly because a suffragan bishop has no seat in the House of Lords.

One other looming event might markedly affect what happens: union with the Methodists. It is certain that Methodists will accept no other bishops except those elected by the Church. They would not (most of them would not) mind bishops presented formally to the queen on election. But they would not like the queen, even without the prime minister, to have a veto, and they could not suffer the prime minister to have any part in the matter whatever. Conceivably the Anglican part of an Anglican-Methodist Church could continue with its system, the Methodist part with its system, and such an idea has been broached. It is incredible in practice. Union with Methodists means an elective system of bishops. Such a change would be natural, and seem to be necessary, and would be procured in the Act of Parliament which provided for the union of the two churches. But whether such elected bishops could have seats in the House of Lords is very doubtful. It is of course not yet certain that there will be any union between the Church of England and the Methodists.

*

Note. The important material, historical as well as actual, is found in the Reports of the Selborne Commission (1916) on Church and State, the Cecil Commission (1935) on Church and State, the Moberly Commission (1952) on Church and State, the Howick Commission (1964) on Crown Appointments and the Chadwick Commission (1970) on Church and State.

Gerard Bartelink

The Use of the Words *Electio* and *Consensus* in the Church until about 600

THE development and local variations in the early Church in the procedure for appointing bishops were paralleled by a development and by local fluctuations in the Latin terminology used. Many terms were current, but, on the one hand, the words *electio/eligere* and, on the other, at least from the fourth century onwards, *consensus/consentire* came to be used increasingly.

Many of the accounts that we have of episcopal appointments are so incomplete and imprecise that the terms used are obscure and this has often resulted in a wrong interpretation of the texts. One example is the juridical term *constituere*, usually applied to the installation of a secular magistrate. When used for the appointment of a bishop, however, it was often equated with *ordinare*, to ordain, although it has a much wider meaning, including ordination. In an episcopal election, the part played by the people alone was frequently expressed by *electio/eligere*, but sometimes the part played by the local clergy and even that played by neighbouring bishops were included in the one term.

The words *constituere* or *instituere* were applied to the appointment of the first bishops by the apostles in the earliest texts, such as Tertullian's *De Praescriptione Haereticorum* 32, 3 ("*ab apostolis in episcopatum constitutos*") and the early Latin translation of Irenaeus' *Adversus Haereses*, 3, 3 ("*qui ab apostolis instituti sunt episcopi*"). The word *consentire* was first used for the consent of the local community in the second-century Latin translation of the first letter of Clement, describing the appointment of bishops by the apostles, 44, 1 ("*igitur illos consti utos ab illis* [i.e., *apostolis*] *vel postmodum a quibusdam viris ornatis consentiente a ecclesia omne"*).

Cyprian used *eligere* for the choice of bishops (*"potestatem vel eligendi dignos sacerdotes vel indignos recusandi"*, *Ep.* 67, 3), but he also used *facere*, which might also refer to the part played by the community in the election (*"sacerdoti quem tanto amore et ardore feciistis"*, *Ep.* 44, 4, 1; *"episcopo semel facto"*, *Ep.* 44, 3, 1) and *constituere*. It is possible that he used three different words for the purpose of stylistic variation (*Ep.* 44, 3, 1). The word *deligere* also occurs, for example, in *Ep.* 44, 2, 1: *"collegae nostri iam delecti et ordinati"*, in which we see a distinction between the acts of choice and of ordination,[1] and in *Ep.* 67, 5, 1: *"ut ... episcopi eiusdem provinciae proximi quique conveniant et episcopus deligatur plebe praesente"*. Later on, however, this use of *deligere* and *eligere* seems to occur purely incidentally (for example, Rufinus' translation of Eusebius, *Hist. eccl.*, 6, 29, 3: *"pro episcopo deligendo"*).

Eligere, however, was the most common term. Its employment for the choice of pagan priests and priestesses[2] was only a parallel usage and the *electio* of the emperor cannot have exerted any lasting influence, because this was hardly mentioned before the third century. (See, for example, Vopiscus, *Vita Aureliani*, 40, 3: *"senatus ... electionem imperatoris in exercitum refudit"*; an apparent beginning can, however, be found in Pliny's panegyric to Trajan.) Other terms, such as *creare*, were used for the election of Roman officials in the republican period and later. It is worth noting too that ἐκλέγεσθαι was translated by *eligere* in cases of the election of priests in the Old Testament, and in the choice of a successor to Judas in Acts 1. 24: *"Tu Domine qui corda nostri omnium, ostende, quem elegeris ex his duobus"*.[3] There is also an element of divine inspiration, the idea that God himself determined the choice by means of man's action, contained in the biblical use of *eligere*, thus enabling an appeal to be made to

[1] J. Gaudemet, *L'Église dans l'Empire romain (IVᵉ–Vᵉ siècles)* (*Histoire du droit et des institutions de l'Église en occident*, 3) (Paris, 1958), p. 330.
[2] The inscription Dessau at Ostia, for example, reads: *"iudicio maiestatis eius* (i.e., *Isidis*) *electo Anubiaco"*.
[3] Cf. 1 Cor. 4. 9 (*Vet. Lat.*): *"noſ Deus apoſ ſ novissimos elegit"*; Ps. Barn. Ep. 5, 9 (*versio vetus*): *"apostolos, quı cipiebant praedicare evangelium suum, elegit"*.

the Bible in the use of this Latin word, which was not possible in Greek, in which ἐκλεγεσθαι was not used for the choice of a bishop.

In the *Vita S. Aniani* 2, for example, a text dating from 1029, but containing many very ancient elements, we read that the Bible was opened at random in a search for scriptural confirmation of the choice of a bishop, and the following passage was found: *"Beatus quem elegisti et assumpsisti, inhabitat in tabernaculis tuis"* (Ps. 64. 5). Other texts also show that an attempt was made to emphasize divine inspiration in such cases of *electio*.

Cyprian did not use *consensus/consentire* to describe the part played by the community in such cases of choice, but *suffragium* and probably *iudicium* and *testimonium* (*"adque intellegant episcopo semel facto et collegarum ac plebis testimonio et iudicio conprobato, alium constitui nullo modo posse"*, *Ep.* 44, 3, 1). He too stressed the view that the consent of the people, particularly unanimous consent, was regarded as God's judgment (*"contra suffragium vestrum et Dei iudicium"*; *"secundum vestra divina suffragia"*, *Ep.* 43, 1). This idea is common in later texts.

From the fourth century onwards, *electio/eligere* was undoubtedly the most usual word for the choice of a bishop and *consensus/consentire* came also to be used more and more frequently. This *consensus* was often expressed in an *acclamatio* (see, for example, Paulinus of Milan, *Vita Ambrosii*, 6; *"Ad cuius vocis sonum totius populi ora conversa sunt acclamantis: 'Ambrosium episcopum' ... in hunc unum mirabili concordia consenserunt"*; Augustine, *Ep.* 213, 1: *"A populo acclamatum est"*; *Avellana Collectio, Ep.* 4: *"in una accalamatione"*). The verb *consentire* seems to have been used in Christian texts before the noun *consensus*, although the latter developed, from about 400 onwards, with great rapidity into a technical term. The expression of the people's *consensus* in an *acclamatio* in the election of an emperor was also a common phenomenon in later antiquity, and we may assume that this influenced the Christian use of the term (see, for example, Iulius Capitolinus, *Vita Maximi et Balbini*, 2, 9: *"post haec acclamatum est uno consensu"*). In this context it is worth while giving some attention to the remarkable historical background to the word *consensus* in connection with appointments and distinctions.

The word *consensus*[4] occurs in the later republican period, and in the imperial period in inscriptions, not in legal enactments or treaties, but rather in dedications and inscriptions of honour containing important decrees, which were emphasized by the consensus, the latter often having an emotional or even religious undertone.[5] It is important to note in this context that the term *consensus* was used in non-Christian texts as confirmation of an official appointment only in the sacral sphere. Whenever the Roman Emperor appealed to the *consensus universorum*, as Augustus did (*Monumentum Ancyranum*, 34), it was not primarily a juridical element that was stressed, but the fact that the consecration that he had received was a higher one than that of a magistrate. Similarly, the words *unanimis consensus* appear in numerous Christian texts pointing to the part played by God. So, too, this unanimity was regarded by non-Christians as something that went back to divine inspiration (see Cassius Dio, *Hist. Rom.*, 75, 4, 4). The Christian use of *consensus/consentire*, then, was clearly influenced by profane traditions.

By the fifth or sixth century, the words *consensus/consentire* had come to replace synonymous expressions almost entirely, and the terminology used in connection with the choice of bishops had become increasingly stereotyped. This process was also paralleled by the decreased importance of the part played by the people in the choice, and an increase in that played by neighbouring bishops (see Gaudemet, *op. cit.*, p. 333). In a fairly early decretal, probably by Pope Damasus and relating to the situation in Gaul in the second half of the fourth century, it is stated that the favour of the people (*favor popularis*) should not be used to become a bishop. Furthermore, the word *testimonium* is employed in this text for the activity of the community: "*non enim*

---

[4] See, for example, the account of the election of Fabian, the bishop of Rome (Rufinus' translation of Eusebius, *Hist. Eccl.*, 6, 29, 4: "*omnes velut uno spiritu commotos hunc esse episcopatu dignum per Dei iudicium decrevisse*"); Leo the Great, *Ep.* 40: "*Postulationis quidem humanae, sed inspirationis credimus fuisse divinae*"; *Liber Diurnus* (Förster, 112): "*non sine divine misericordiae nutu*"; Gregory of Tours (*Hist. Franc.*, 4, 15), discussing the confirmation of an episcopal election by a Frankish prince: "*Respondit rex ... Fiat voluntas Dei et beati Martini, compleatur electio*".

[5] See H. Instinsky, "*Consensus universorum*", *Hermes*, 75 (1940), pp. 265–278.

*quid populus velit, sed quid evangelica disciplina perquiritur;
plebs tunc habet testimonium quotiens ad digni alicuius meritum
reprehendens* (proceeding from the merits) *auram favoris imper-
tit"* (ed. Babut).

Although it is rather tendentious, the *Avellana Collectio* provides a number of important terminological data especially with
regard to the election of the bishop of Rome in the second half
of the fourth and the beginning of the fifth century. It is clear
from *Ep.* 17, A.D. 417, addressed to Emperor Honorius and fav-
ouring the choice of Boniface as the bishop of Rome, that the
term *consensus* still had no fixed meaning—the election took
place *"acclamatione totius populi et consensu meliorum civitatis".* Obviously, then, the *consensus* is separated here from the
acclamatio and limited to the notable people in the city.

In *Ep.* 37, a decree from Emperor Honorius outlining the rules
that he proposed for the election, *divinum iudicium* is separated
from the *universitatis consensus: "sed illum in sede divina per-
mansurum, quem ex numero clericorum nova ordinatione
divinum iudicium et universitatis censensus elegerit".* Iudicium,
of course, refers to the candidature proposed by the bishops, which
is known as *divinum* in so far as God's judgment is manifested
in it. In addition to this, the universal *consensus* also forms part
of the *electio.* In this text, the *consensus* refers to the consent of
all those concerned, but, whenever it is only a question of a *consensus* of the people, the local clergy are usually also included.

The local clergy were, however, sometimes mentioned separ-
ately—for example, in a letter from Pope Celestine in 428:
*"Nullus invitis detur episcopus. Cleri, plebis et ordinis consensus
et desiderium requiratur"* (Migne, *PL,* 56, 579). The word
desiderium occurs frequently at this time in connection with *consensus,* as do *petitio/petere* and *postulatio/postulare;*[6] Leo the
Great, *Ep.* 14: *"Cum ergo de summi sacerdotis electione tracta-
bitur, ille omnibus praeponatur quem cleri plebisque consensus
concorditer postularit"* (Migne, *PL,* 54, 673). There are also clear
parallels in profane texts from the beginning of the imperial

[6] See J. Gaudemet, *op. cit.,* pp. 330–8; F. L. Ganshof, "Note sur l'élection
des évêques dans l'empire romain au IV*e* et pendant la première moitié du
V*e* siècle", in *Mélanges Fernand de Visscher,* 3 (Brussels, 1950), pp. 330–8;
see also *petere* in Sulpicius Severus, *Vita Martini,* 9, 1.

period of this terminology used in connection with *consensus* (see *Corp. Inscr. Lat.* XII, 1585: *"ex consensu et postulatione populi"*; *ibid.*, XIV, 3014: *"postulante populo"*).

The sixth-century Gallic terminology, which had clearly become quite fixed, is reflected in Gregory of Tours' *Historia Francorum*. The only term used, for example, for the choice of bishops is *electio/eligere*. In his very incomplete reports, Gregory strongly emphasizes the part played by the people—*"a clero et omni populo electus"*, 4, 35; *"Gregorium diaconem plebs omnis elegit"*, 10, 1; cf. *Traditio Apostolica, versio latina*, Tidner, 119: *"Episcopus ordinetur electus ab omni populo"* and the *Statuta ecclesiae antiqua*, Munier, 78: *"consensu clericorum et laicorum et convenu totius provinciae episcoporum maximeque metropolitani vel auctoritate vel praesentia ordinetur episcopus."*

According to the *Historia Francorum*, a development took place in the meaning of the word *consensus* (the neuter form *consensum* also occurs). It may mean not only "consent", but also "charter", "decree" or "written, unanimous petition" (called *decretum* in the *Liber Diurnus*), sent to the prince for his confirmation. This specialized meaning seems to have been confined to Gaul. A good example of a *unanimous* petition of this kind (*"generale prece"*, *"cunctorum voce"*) can be found in the *Marculfi Formulae*, I, 7 (ed. Uddholm, 50). The same narrower meaning is also found in the *Historia Francorum*, 4, 26: *"consensum fecerunt in Heraclium ... presbyterum, quod regi ... transmiserunt"*; 8.22: *"cum muneribus et consensu civium ad regem properat"*; 10, 1, in connection with the election of Gregory the Great, the bishop of Tours using a term current in Gaul for a situation in Rome, where the official word was *decretum*: *"praefectum urbis Romae ... consensum, quod populus fecerat, imperatori direxit"*. This development in the meaning of the word *consensus* is paralleled in a process by which the meaning became more concrete—something which occurred at a later period in the case of *electio* ("election document); see, for example, Rodolfus Monachus, *Vita S. Lietberti Cameracensis Episcopi*, 18 (1076): *"recitatur electio et testificatur a cunctis"* (Migne, *PL*, 146, 1459C).

The *Liber Diurnus* also contains a number of important texts, in which *consensus/consentire* occurs most frequently to indicate unanimity in the choice of a bishop; see, for instance, Förster, 112, the election of Gregory the Great, 594: *"ita post mortem summi pontificis in unius electione omnium vota concurrere et convenire consensus ut nullus penitus inveniretur qui discors possit existere".* The word *consensus* is paraphrased as *unanimis consonantia* (144) and is varied stylistically by the use of *assensus* (112). (The term *lectio*, which occurs alongside *electio*, 115, is probably also a stylistic variant.) *Assensus* also occurs in other texts, where it is synonymous with *consensus*, for example, in Hilar(i)us Papa, *Ep.* 16, 4, 3, Thiel, 162: *"Nam plerique sacerdotes in mortis confinio constituti in locum suum feruntur alios designatis nominibus subrogare: ut scilicet non legitima expectetur electio, sed defuncti gratificatio pro populi habeatur assensu".*

It is clear from the additions to *electio/eligere* in the *Liber Diurnus* that serious attempts were made to suppress the purely human juridical element in episcopal elections and stress the aspect of divine inspiration. Examples of this are *"ut . . . caelestis dignatio demonstraret, quem dignum . . . iubeat eligendum* (115); *"Deo dedicata electio"* (118); *"Dei gratia electus"* (148). Moreover, the close connection between *electio* and *consensus* is illustrated in the formula that recurs again and again, a formula in which *electio* figures as the subject of the verb *consentire* (144 and elsewhere): *"in personam . . . Deo cooperante et beatorum apostolorum annisu concurrit atque consensit electio".* The formula *electo consentiens,* occurring in one form or another at the end of election documents in the *Liber Diurnus* as evidence of individual consent, is another indication of the close link between the two terms; see, for instance, *"electo nostro consentiens subscripsi* (113 and elsewhere); *Avellana Collectio, Ep.* 37: *"quem . . . consensus elegerit".*

Finally, it is interesting to note that there is a great similarity between the terminology used by Gregory the Great and that used in the *Liber Diurnus*; for example, *"omnium vestrum in Constantio convenisse consensum", Ep.* 3, 29; *"in persona Iohannis . . . consensum omnium vestrum et . . . principis convenisse . . . voluntatem", Ep.* 5, 10. Gregory also placed great emphasis on the *consensus* in the *electio,* for instance, in formulae such as *"communi sensu eligere; uno eodemque consensu; in electione unanimiter consensisse"*.

Even the very small selection of texts that I have quoted in this article can give us quite a clear idea of how the terms used in the choice and appointment of bishops developed in the course of the early Christian centuries into rather stereotyped formulae, with the words *electio/eligere* and *consensus/consentire* occupying a central place. The first was later employed in connection with the election, not of Roman officials, but of the emperors, but there is no question of its having had priority here over the Christian use of the term. There is, however, an important relationship between it and a number of biblical texts which was often conscious and in which a part was played by the desire to stress divine inspiration. The relationship between the second of the two terms and profane usage, especially in connection with the election of emperors, is more pronounced. Used in the profane context of distinctions and dedications, *consensus* undoubtedly had emotional undertones. In Christian usage, the word was frequently employed together with *acclamatio* and the custom of seeking the consensus of the community gained legal status and was expressed in various enactments. In this way, it came to have a certain juridical validity, perhaps the best example of this being the developed meaning that it acquired in Gaul as a "written, unanimous petition".

Translated by David Smith

Biographical Notes

GERARD BARTELINK was born in 1924. Doctor of classical philology, he has been scientific assistant for Latin and Greek Palaeo-Christian studies at the University of Nijmegen since 1966. Among his published works are: *Lexicologisch-semantische studie over de taal van de Apostolische Vaders* (Nijmegen, 1952), *Etymologisering bij Vergilius* (Amsterdam, 1965), *Geschiedenis van de klassieke letterkunde* (Utrecht-Antwerp, 1971²).

ANTONY BLACK was born in 1936 in Leeds. He studied at Shrewsbury School and at King's College, Cambridge. Master of arts and doctor of history, he is reader of political science at the University of Dundee.

OWEN CHADWICK was born in 1916. He studied at Cambridge University. He has been professor of modern history at Cambridge University since 1968 and was president of the Church and State Commission 1966–1970. Among his published works are: *The Reformation* (1971⁶) and *The Victorian Church* (2 vols., 1971²).

ENRIQUE DUSSEL was born 24 December 1934 at La Paz (Argentine) and is a Catholic. He studied at the National University of Cuyo and, in Europe, at the Universities of Louvain, Mainz, Münster, Madrid and the Sorbonne and at the Institut Catholique (Paris). Doctor of philosophy, doctor of the University (Paris, Sorbonne) and licentiate of theology he is professor of history and of philosophy at the Latin-American Pastoral Institute, Quito, Ecuador, and professor of ethics at the National University of Cuyo. Among his published works is: *Hipótesis para una historia de la Iglesia en América Latina* (1967; 2nd edn. under the title *América Latina en la historia de la salvación: 1492–1971*—Barcelona, 1972).

BRUNO KLEINHEYER was born 22 April 1923 at Hüls/Krefeld (Germany) and ordained in 1953. He studied at the Universities of Bonn, Tübingen and Munich and at the Faculty of Theology in Trèves. Doctor of theology, he is professor of practical theology (liturgy) at the University of Regensburg. Among his published works are: *Die Priesterweihe im römischen Ritus* (Trèves, 1962) and *Erneuerung des Hochgebetes* (Regensburg, 1969).

WILHELM KÖLMEL was born in 1909. He is a *Privatdozent* at the University of Munich in the history of the Middle Ages and of modern times and director of a lyceum (Gymnasium) in E tlingen/Baden. Among his published works are: *W. Ockham und seine kirchenpolitischen Schriften* and *Regimen Christianum*. He has also written many articles on Church-State relations and on the history of humanism.

JEAN LECLERCQ, O.S.B., was born 31 January 1911 in Avesnes (France) and ordained in 1936. Doctor of theology and doctor *h.c.* of the Catholic Universities of Milan and Louvain, he is a professor at the Institute "Lumen Vitae" (Brussels) and at the Gregorian University (Rome) and a corresponding member of the British Academy. Among his published works is: *The Spirituality of the Middle Ages* (London, 1968).

BERNARD PLONGERON was born 5 March 1931 in Meaux and ordained in 1964. He studied at the Sorbonne and at the Faculty of Theology, Paris. Doctor of theology and doctor of history, he is a lecturer at the Institut Catholique, Paris, in charge of research at the National Centre of Scientific Research and director of programmes of the Centre of Research of Religious History (Paris). Among his published works is: *Conscience religieuse en Révolution—Regards sur l'historiographie religieuse de la Révolution française* (Paris, 1969).

ROBERT TRISCO was born 11 November 1929 in Chicago and ordained in 1954. He studied at the Gregorian University (Rome). Licentiate of theology and doctor of the history of the Church, he is associate professor of the history of the Church at the Catholic University of America. He is also secretary of the American Catholic Historical Association and editor of the *Catholic Historical Review*.

WALTER ULLMANN was born 29 November 1910. He studied at many Universities, notably at Cambridge, Munich, Vienna and Innsbruck. Docteur ès lettres, doctor of law and of canon law, he is professor of medieval ecclesiastical history at Cambridge University, visiting professor at Johns Hopkins University, fellow of Trinity College, Cambridge, and a member of the British Academy. He has been president of the Ecclesiastical History Society and is vice-president of the Henry Bradshaw Society. He is also general editor of "Cambridge Studies in Medieval Life and Thought". Among his published works are: *The Medieval Idea of Law, The Origins of the Great Schism*.

ANTON WEILER was born 6 November 1927 in Voorburg (Holland). He studied at the Jesuit Faculty of Philosophy, at the University of Nijmegen and at the École des Chartes and the École des Hautes Études in Paris. Docteur ès lettres, he is professor of medieval history and of paleography at the University of Nijmegen. He is the author of the section concerned with medieval history in *Geschiedenis van de Kerk in Nederland* (Utrecht, 1963²). Among his published lectures are: *Humanism en Scholastiek in de Renaissance-Tijd* and *Nicolas van Cues en de oecumenische problematiek voor de Reformatie*